ENCAMPMENT

RESISTANCE, GRACE, AND AN
UNHOUSED COMMUNITY

MAGGIE HELWIG

COACH HOUSE BOOKS, TORONTO

first edition

Canada Council   Conseil des Arts   Canadä
for the Arts   du Canada

ONTARIO ARTS COUNCIL
CONSEIL DES ARTS DE L'ONTARIO   Ontario
an Ontario government agency
un organisme du gouvernement de l'Ontario

Published with the generous assistance of the Canada Council for the Arts
and the Ontario Arts Council. Coach House Books also acknowledges the
support of the Government of Canada through the Canada Book Fund and
the Government of Ontario through the Ontario Book Publishing Tax Credit.

LIBRARY AND ARCHIVES CANADA CATALOGUING IN PUBLICATION

Title: Encampment : resistance, grace, and an unhoused community / Maggie
Helwig.
Names: Helwig, Maggie, 1961- author
Description: First edition.
Identifiers: Canadiana (print) 20250113732 | Canadiana (ebook)
2025011660X | ISBN 9781552455043 (softcover) | ISBN 9781770568549
(PDF) | ISBN 9781770568426 (EPUB)
Subjects: LCSH: Helwig, Maggie, 1961- | LCSH: Homeless camps—Onta-
rio—Toronto. | LCSH: Homelessness—Ontario—Toronto. | LCSH: Church
work with the homeless—Ontario—Toronto. | LCSH: Social justice—Onta-
rio—Toronto. | LCSH: Homeless persons—Ontario—Toronto—Biography.
| LCSH: Political activists—Canada—Biography. | LCGFT: Biographies.
Classification: LCC HV4510.T6 H45 2025 | DDC 362.5/9209713541—dc23

Encampment: Resistance, Grace, and an Unhoused Community is available as
an ebook: ISBN 978 1 77056 842 6 (EPUB), 978 1 77056 854 9 (PDF)

PRAISE FOR *ENCAMPMENT*

'In crystalline prose, [*Encampment*] sheds light on not only the struggles of the unhoused but the heartlessness of a society that would rather not see them at all.'
— *Publishers Weekly*, ★ **Starred Review**

'Helwig's *Encampment* is an urgent call for compassion, part memoir, part homily. In eloquent prose it takes us on Helwig's journey as Anglican priest and activist into complex engagement with city staff, lawyers, politicians, and the unhoused community she works tirelessly to learn from and assist.'
— **Martha Baillie, author of** *There is No Blue*

'Helwig is a priest, human rights activist, poet, caregiver, friend, mother, Mother. And she is, most admirably, a reader – a reader of sacred texts, yes, but also a reader of a city, of a neighbourhood, of bureaucracy, of poetry, of law by turns incensing and nonsensical, and of a community frequently deemed illegible or illegitimate in their living because the living looks different. With this book, Helwig maps a space for difference. *Encampment* enacts the gesture of a hand reaching out to meet another, of a question being formed, and of a need – however difficult to translate its utterance – that is listened to with respect and responded to with attention. Reader to reader, Helwig asks us: How might we better live together?'
— **Claire Foster, Type Books**

'If you have seen a homeless person or an encampment and wondered who, why, or how, this is the book for you. Maggie

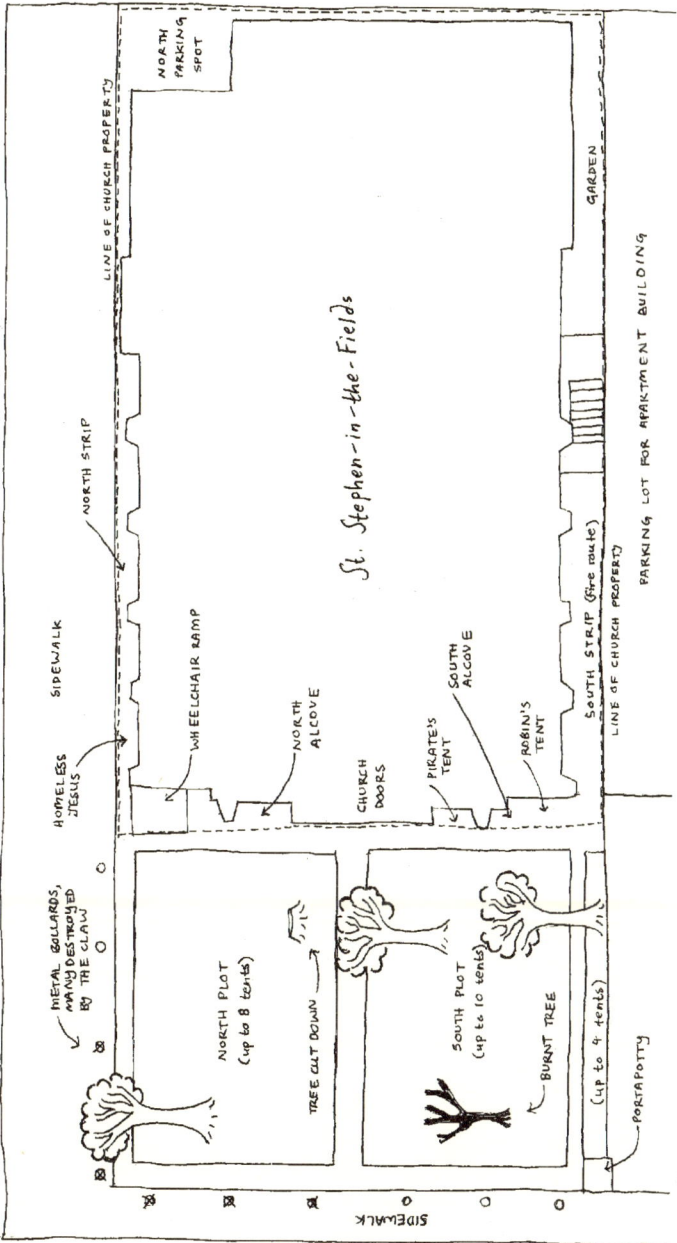

CAMPBELL RUSSELL LANE

COLLEGE STREET

LINE OF CHURCH PROPERTY

NORTH PARKING SPOT

NORTH STRIP

SIDEWALK

WHEELCHAIR RAMP

HOMELESS JESUS

METAL BOLLARDS, MANY DESTROYED BY THE CLAW

NORTH PLOT (up to 8 tents)

TREE CUT DOWN

St. Stephen-in-the-Fields

NORTH ALCOVE

CHURCH DOORS

PIRATE'S TENT

SOUTH ALCOVE

ROBIN'S TENT

SOUTH PLOT (up to 10 tents)

BURNT TREE

SOUTH STRIP (fire route)

LINE OF CHURCH PROPERTY

GARDEN

PARKING LOT FOR APARTMENT BUILDING

PORTA POTTY

(up to 4 tents)

SIDEWALK

BELLEVUE AVENUE

Here

It is a secure place, both in the sense that it is indestructible and in the sense that it is safe for the most vulnerable.

– Rowan Williams

One day, as I was starting to write this book, I was leaving the church where I work when an angry woman stopped me, after throwing a bag of garbage into the encampment in our yard, and told me that a person had started sleeping in her yard, and that I needed to tell her how she could find out who it was and make him go away. I suggested that she ask the person himself who he was.

She stared at me as if I had suggested that she fly to the moon for information, and exclaimed, 'But he takes drugs!'

'You can still ask him who he is,' I said.

And she stormed away up the street.

I tell this story not primarily to illustrate how I have come to be seen as responsible for all homeless people within about an eight-block radius of the church, although that is, for some reason, true. I tell it because there is a great gulf fixed, and very few people are willing to cross it. People who have not lived in the world of which encampments are part are afraid, and they are angry. And they cannot imagine that there is a way to cross that line, to speak to a homeless person as a fellow human being, without somehow themselves being harmed, being damaged, being touched by a world they would rather deny. A kinder, more well-intentioned, neighbour once told me he didn't want to introduce himself to encampment residents, because if they knew he lived nearby, they might knock on his door all the time asking for help. It seems like a reasonable fear, and it is hard to explain that unhoused people have such deep and well-founded apprehensions about the housed world that, even when they are living against the wall of the church, and even when they know we are an institution that is here to support them, it is almost always my job to go out the door and identify need.

I am writing this because I want you to understand my world, the world I live in, and the world I live alongside. I have been an Anglican priest since 2012; I have been the priest at St. Stephen-in-the-Fields, in Kensington Market in Toronto, since 2013. We have had, I guess somewhat famously, an encampment in our churchyard since about the spring of 2022, although there was no single clear point when it began, and it is tied up with events and choices going back for years, and is perhaps ultimately the responsibility of the poet and theologian Rowan Williams, who was once the Archbishop of Canterbury. I am writing this because I want you to understand that this is a world of real people, who struggle and are kind, who are often special and beautiful in ways that most of our society cannot and does not try to understand. I want you to understand that I have felt safer here than in most other places, hard as it has sometimes been.

It is a different world, and why I am easy with this world is hard to pin down. Because it is honest, and most people are not honest. Because I have waged my own lifelong battles with depression, anxiety, OCD, probably undiagnosed autism, and because I was viciously bullied through my whole school career and took on board the clear message that the normal world didn't want me, and I decided fairly early on that I didn't want them either. Because my parents taught drama and creative writing in the prisons, and there were social dynamics I met as a child that most middle-class people learn in training workshops as adults, if they learn them at all. Because at one point in my twenties, I looked at a man panhandling at Bloor and Bathurst, and thought that I needed to take completely seriously the proposition that he was Jesus. Because my autistic daughter has spent most of her twenty-eight years being expelled from program after program. Because I don't dress very well, and my hair isn't very good, and I look more like I belong in the world of the encampment than in the world of the others. Because people on the street, exhausting as they can often be, have also been kind to me, and to my daughter, more consistently than almost anyone else. Because there are reasons I probably don't even know.

And I am writing this because I do not have much optimism about what is coming in our society, in our world. We are standing at the edge of catastrophic climate breakdown and the fall of a long empire, and all the collateral damage which the fall of an empire brings. Nothing stable is going to last; and the only way that we, the small and the ordinary, might survive in any decent way is if we learn to take care of each other, to do it deeply and consistently and in ways that will change how we think and how we live. This is one story, flawed and incomplete, of people who have been trying to look after each other in very hard times, and some of the ways in which we have been changed.

And I am writing this because if you want to know who someone is, you can ask them.

❦

In some Indigenous traditions, you are not supposed to play or sing a drum song for the community until the song has been given to you by another drummer. The giving of a song is a sacred act and a sacred trust, and you must be responsible to that song.

In the same way, the stories I will tell you are stories I have been given: not always formally, but by the terms of long relationships. I have a profound responsibility to these stories, a responsibility to tell them, and to tell them as truly as I can. There are other stories I cannot tell you, although they underlie some parts of this book, because they are not mine to tell.

Sometimes I have used real names, and sometimes I have not. In the cases of church volunteers and encampment residents, I have used real names when people gave me permission to do so; otherwise, names have been changed. I have not indicated which names are real and which have been changed, in part to help protect the privacy of people for whom this is important.

In the case of City staff and politicians, I have used the real names of those who hold elected office and are by definition public figures. City staff are usually not referred to by their real names.

This is, of course, a book about Toronto, and many of the details are specific to the ways in which social services are managed in Toronto. But the large picture is common to nearly all cities now, and increasingly to towns as well, and rural areas face struggles that are not unconnected. The crises of displacement, poverty, and toxic drugs, the transformation of housing into a luxury good, the apparently terminal fraying of the social fabric: these are not unique to Toronto. They are part, now, of everyone's world, and all of us must decide how we are going to respond.

❦

We think, maybe, that homelessness is some kind of stable state, like being housed except without housing. Without really considering it, most people imagine that people who are homeless live in, if not one place, at least in one condition, that their days are in some way predictable. But homelessness is, more than anything else, a life of constant displacement.

You couch-surf sometimes. You may have lived for a while in one of the increasingly few cheap rooming houses, but more and more they are being torn down, or renovated into expensive large homes. Maybe you used to live at the Waverley Hotel, before it became a condo development, or one of the other vanishing long-stay hotels. Maybe you've been renovicted from a basement in the Market (in Toronto, a landlord can kick you out if they say they're going to renovate your unit). Or maybe your parents just threw you out, for any of the reasons that might happen. Maybe a relationship has broken down. Maybe you suddenly lost a job, or spent a month in such a deep depression that you didn't, or couldn't, meet a rent payment.

Remember that if you rely on government support – here in Toronto, Ontario Works (OW) or the Ontario Disability Support Program (ODSP) – your income is so low that even doubling it instantly would leave you far below the poverty line. Remember that we have chosen, as a society, to set social assistance rates at a fraction of what we acknowledge is necessary to survive; that, essentially, to be on social assistance – to be disabled, to be old, to be laid off and looking for work – is to be told that you don't really deserve to live. Certainly not to live indoors.

Current calculations suggest that you need a gross income of at least $64,000 a year to afford rent on a one-bedroom apartment in Toronto – which currently averages around $2,400 per month, and was around $3,000 per month during the period of time covered by this book. The maximum OW payment for a single person is $8,796 *per year.* ODSP is slightly better – a single person might get as much as $16,416 per year, though not everyone on ODSP gets that much. A single minimum-wage earner, working forty hours every week, could theoretically earn as much as $35,776 per year, before deductions. None of these people would be even close to achieving a bachelor – much less a one-bedroom – apartment, at market rent, unless they are among the handful of lucky people who moved into rent-controlled units long ago. Some other cities might be better, but not by much.

Even much 'affordable' housing is far out of reach. As of March 2024, Habitat for Humanity, which builds affordable housing, was advertising for families with yearly incomes between $90,000 and $130,000. That same month I, as the parent of a disabled adult who lives with me, received a listing for new 'affordable' units, and it was, in fact, the case that my full-time professional salary put us in the qualifying range for this act of charity. The monthly rent for the smallest unit far exceeded the full amount of a monthly ODSP payment, and a family with two full-time minimum-wage earners would not have enough income to qualify to apply.

You are probably trying to get onto the list for the small amount of genuine rent-geared-to-income housing that exists in Toronto, much of it run by the notorious City-run Toronto Community Housing, but you can't be classified as 'housing ready' and able to go on that list until you have an income source – probably ODSP – as well as valid ID and several years of completed income tax returns. If all your ID has been stolen, which it almost certainly has at some point, you need to start from scratch. You may not have done your income tax for years – why would you, when you have little or no income? Why would you make it a priority when your whole life is stress and disruption? And you may have no idea how to start. By now, you probably have high enough levels of anxiety and depression that even getting to an ID clinic becomes an insurmountable challenge.

Not only that, but in order to be officially 'chronically homeless' and therefore given a degree of priority for rent-geared-to-income housing, you are required to have spent some amount of time (usually six months in the past year) in a shelter, either one which is City-run or which submits data to the City's central database. If not – if you have been sleeping on the street, or in a tent, or in the stairwell of a shop, for instance, or even on your cousin's floor in an overcrowded apartment – you are not officially homeless for purposes of housing access. Under certain circumstances, if you have spent a shorter amount of time in a shelter, or regularly visited one of the drop-ins that sends statistics to the central database (many drop-ins do not), and if you have regular contact with Streets to Homes, you might be able to get a caseworker to write a letter stating that you have indeed been homeless for six months or more, but if you have not appeared in the database at all, as some haven't, even a caseworker's letter isn't enough to allow you to be prioritized. Most homeless people don't understand this arcane system, which seems to have been created to protect against a very notional and improbable kind of fraud – I barely understand it myself. But it is yet another barrier against even beginning to access housing.

Very possibly, you are already on the waiting list, but whether you are officially homeless, or homeless without official recognition, or just living in some kind of precarious and unsafe indoor accommodation, the wait will be long. One of my colleagues recently reported that someone she works with had just qualified for a rent-geared-to-income unit (or rather, for an opportunity to view photographs of a unit, and accept or decline it based on that) for the first time. He had been on the waiting list for eighteen years.

You may spend time in shelters or shelter-hotels – if you can even get into one, which is a whole other problem – but you may not feel safe there: there is widespread infectious disease, there is likely violence, there is certainly theft. And these institutions have stringent 'service restriction' policies, which means you can be evicted at a moment's notice for reasons you may not know or understand, reasons that can sometimes be as trivial as smoking in a stairwell or missing the nightly bed check. You can be restricted for breaking rules you didn't even know existed. Or you haven't broken the rules, but maybe you can't be with your partner, or your pet; maybe there is a stairway you can technically climb, but only in pain. You are evicted, or you leave. Service restrictions may prevent you from going into any other shelter for some time, or, if your records are not updated at the central database, as they frequently are not, you may be considered still 'in shelter' and so not eligible to go anywhere else.

Maybe you go into hospital with an infection, because bad infections are hard to avoid when you don't have a place to wash cuts and wounds, or basic first aid supplies like antibiotic ointments, and your space is gone when you come out. Or perhaps one of your workers, because by now you probably have several workers and you may not even know them very well, decides that you should be 'formed' – held in the hospital briefly under the Mental Health Act. This might last twenty-four or forty-eight or even seventy-two hours, but it won't last longer than that, because there is almost no public provision for longer-term mental health care. But in the meantime, you may have lost a space you were holding, indoors or outdoors, and you have probably lost possessions, maybe your phone, maybe your ID.

Sometimes you miss a court appearance, because you're in the hospital perhaps, or you can't figure out how to get to the court, or you're afraid of the courts and have no one to support you, and then perhaps there is a bench warrant issued, and you spend some time in jail. Maybe not long, but again, long enough to lose a place, your things, maybe your dog, anything stable that you might rely on. What was the original charge? It can be hard to remember, when the 'failure to appear' cycle becomes almost self-sustaining, but it may have been as small as failing to pay a fine for panhandling, or riding your bicycle through a red light, or drinking alcohol in public. Maybe you were required to pay the cost of your own eviction process, and defaulted on that payment, and that began a saga of court dates that became self-propelling.

Maybe you have a child, maybe the child is in the custody of your family or of foster parents, maybe you are allowed to see them or not, maybe you struggle to meet the conditions that will allow you to see your child, and then you fail, and then your heart is shattered one more time. Maybe you try to work, but if anyone will hire you without a fixed address, it will be grey economy and unpredictable, and you can be easily replaced for any reason or no reason at all.

Maybe you set up a tent, alone or with others – it's important to know that people were living in tents in Toronto long before the pandemic, though less visibly, mostly in the ravines or under the highway bridges – and then the tent is cleared away one day when you're not there, and again you have lost everything.

And people think 'mental illness,' and they think 'drugs,' and these things are true as well, but they are true in part because the constant background noise of life is displacement and fear, and loss after loss after endless loss.

About getting into a shelter. On any given night, close to ten thousand people will be sleeping in emergency shelters of some kind in Toronto. This is not even close to a full census of the number of people who are homeless – the real number, including couch-surfers and people sleeping rough, could be as much as double that figure. But it serves as some indication of how huge, and how overloaded, the shelter system has become.

In Toronto, the only access to a shelter bed (with the exception of a very few private shelters, mostly run by evangelical Christians) is through a phone number called Central Intake, run by the City. The 'easy listening' hold music for Central Intake is now the best-known piece of music for anyone who works in the field. One of my colleagues was doing a shift in the emergency room one night, and was there when a tiny elderly nun was admitted, over her own protests that she was perfectly fine. As he passed her cubicle later, he heard the Central Intake hold music, and recognized immediately that the little nun was working from her hospital bed to find a bed for someone else. If you call Central Intake, you are likely to sit on hold, listening to the music, for an hour or so. If you do get through, it is not likely to go well.

One of the hidden facts of the system is that many, many shelter beds are permanently unavailable. The 'emergency' shelter system became a long-term home for many people, especially working-age and senior men, a decade or more ago. People have lived in these dormitories for years, and have no prospect of ever moving out. So quite a significant number of beds are ruled out before anyone even starts looking.

A number of years ago, it was possible to phone Central Intake and be offered a bed fairly consistently, but almost always, if you were a man, that bed would be at the Seaton House shelter, universally known on the street as Satan House. The only people willing to accept beds at Satan House were new arrivals to Toronto, who hadn't yet been told about it. But this is irrelevant now, it doesn't happen anymore.

More recently, there was another last-ditch option that might be offered. 129 Peter Street was built as an administrative headquarters for Streets to Homes, the City agency that was created, as the name suggests, to connect homeless people with housing. Given the lack of housing, it soon turned into an agency that connected people with shelter beds, and as the shelters went further and further over capacity, the Streets to Homes workers have found themselves, most days, with nothing to offer but granola bars and bottled water, and on bad days not even granola bars. 129 Peter is primarily office space but has a few referral beds on the top floor. The actual beds are rarely available – though I did once get a woman into one of them by taking her there in a car late at night. But the chairs in the lobby were, for a while, a de facto shelter, so that would be where Central Intake might suggest that people go. Even more recently, we have had the operators at Central Intake suggest to us that people might go and stand outside 129 Peter Street and wait to see if a chair might be vacated during the night. Eventually, even that stopped, and the nearly invariable response from Central Intake became, 'call back in a few hours and check again.' If you have no phone of your own, and no way you can stay near someone who does have a phone, you are out of luck. Even if you do, it could be days. Maybe you could sleep outside 129 Peter Street while you wait, but the sidewalk there is pretty crowded with sleeping people now.

Central Intake does track the number of people it turns away every night. The number varies – from as few as 30 people a night in the winter of 2022 to a staggering 291 people a night, every night, in October 2023, the month during which the church was trying to get a legal injunction to protect the encampment. The numbers are usually lowest in January and February, when a few low-barrier warming centres open up. In January 2024, the average was nearly 150 callers per night turned away without shelter. Through the summer of 2024, the number hovered just above 230.

For a few winters, there were buses that could move people from 129 Peter Street to shelters, or from a warming centre that was full to one that was open. By December 2023, it was clear to the Toronto Transit Commission (TTC) that there was no longer any place for the buses to take people, and there would not be any time soon. So, every night, five buses parked at the Spadina subway station, and people got onto the buses and slept there. We heard rumours about the shelter buses at Spadina for a month before the *Toronto Star* broke the story, and we were afraid that the coverage might mean an end to the program, but it didn't, because there was simply nothing at all that could possibly replace it.

By the time someone arrives in an encampment, they have been living like this for months or, often enough, for years. Some people come just for the time it takes them to get a shelter bed or a shelter-hotel room, which may be just a few days or weeks, but they have to live somewhere in the meantime. Some find friends or family who will let them crash for a while, but that's not a long-term solution either. Some people are still trying to get onto the housing list; some people are already on the list but caught in the interminable wait time. Some people have given up, or been so damaged they cannot trust again that anyone will have their best interests at heart.

One person who slept for a long time in our encampment had been evicted from Toronto Community Housing after a psychotic break, but was still, a year later, listed in the central database as 'housed,' so no one would or could offer them a shelter bed. Another person had fled a Toronto Community Housing apartment when it was taken over by a gang, and was in the official rehousing process, but could not go into a shelter without losing the housing portion of their ODSP payment, which they needed for the rehousing to happen. Another person was renovicted from a basement apartment in the Annex and arrested when they tried to go back for their belongings. Some people who have stayed in the encampment have been employed, usually in precarious shift work in the food industry, but unable to afford even the most basic housing within commuting distance of their jobs. One person was in the encampment for nearly a full year simply because they had lost the keys to their Toronto Community Housing apartment, and didn't know how to get new keys, and couldn't find anyone at the City who could help them with that one simple thing. And another had slept in doorways and parks around the neighbourhood for a decade, was restricted from every shelter and respite, bounced in and out of hospital and jail, moved into a tent in the Grange Park encampment, and came to us after someone tried to set that tent on fire and nearly killed them.

And if you live in this world, everyone understands all of these things – they aren't secret, they are basic knowledge. But if you live outside, in the world of people who are housed and relatively comfortable, people whose anguish and confusion can be concealed behind socially acceptable facades, it is arcane, mysterious. It doesn't seem to make sense because it doesn't make sense, because the system is a Lewis Carroll fantasia, but if you live on the outside, that can be a hard thing to believe. It isn't what the City will tell you – although some City staffers will, in private, if they trust you. What I am telling you, I have learned over years of day-to-day experience, and only because people have shared their lives with me in a way that I have had no right to expect.

❦

The City of Toronto may appear to be the main antagonist in this book, because it is the level of government that directly delivers housing, shelter, and most social services (although not social assistance payments, which are provincially controlled and administered). But I am keenly aware that municipalities in Ontario are also the least resourced level of government, barred by provincial legislation from running a deficit budget, highly limited in the tools they're allowed to use to generate income, and yet charged with tremendous, expensive, life-or-death responsibilities.

This is not an accident. Successive Conservative provincial governments – interrupted by a spell of Liberal governments whose terms were, under Dalton McGuinty, ineffective, and under Kathleen Wynne, frustrated and far too short – have systematically starved municipalities of resources while downloading more and more services, knowing that when everything fell apart, as it inevitably would, it would be the city governments that would be blamed.

So I do have sympathy for the municipal politicians and staff who are trying to function in this dilemma. I know that they have, ultimately, only a little bit more power than I do myself. I know that the municipal government has created more housing in Toronto than the provincial or federal governments, despite far more limited resources; this was already true under Mayor John Tory, and has become more true under Mayor Olivia Chow.

If there is a single thing I would ask from the City of Toronto in this crisis, it is honesty. Too many politicians, and to an even greater extent, far too many City staff, still insist on speaking and behaving as if everything is somehow okay, as if the shelters are not constantly overflowing, as if food banks are not all on the verge of collapsing under unsustainable demand, as if hospitals aren't on their knees, as if homelessness and encampments and hunger and desperation are all, somehow, the result of bad choices by thousands and thousands of the least powerful individuals.

It is a great and frightening thing to face, that the good you want to do may be impossible. Some City councillors have faced it, and bravely done what they could nonetheless. Some City staff have worked on the ground with tremendous compassion and clarity of vision, especially some of the frontline workers at Streets to Homes. But many others have resorted to indifference, to bitterness, or to a wholly unrealistic clinging to the notion that we can make things all right by making 'difficult' people behave. Many, especially in the Encampment Office, have spoken in ways that pass this belief on to the public in general, and have made it very much harder to communicate the systemic failures to those who aren't being immediately hurt by them. Sometimes they have, for whatever reasons, refused to do good that they are able to do, and for this they must be accountable.

But finally, although this is a story of a small number of people and their relationships to a tiny piece of land outside a tiny church, it is driven by greater powers and principalities; by the relentless machine of late capitalism, which devours and discards anyone who is not an efficient economic actor (meaning, sooner or later, all of us), which sets individual self-interest and competition for resources above all else, and structures the economy so that debt and poverty are not only widespread but actually necessary for economic 'health.' This is the storm in which we live right now; this is the flood that each one of us is trying to survive.

Wilderness

St. Stephen-in-the-Fields seems like a strange name for a church at the northern edge of the extremely urban neighbourhood of Kensington Market. It is a remnant, in fact, from its earliest days, when the little brick Gothic building went up on the grounds of the estate of the Denisons, who were career military, part of the Family Compact, and probably among the last slaveowners in Canada, and whose descendants, even to this day, phone me when family members die, taking for granted that we are their family church and will bury them, though they are strangers to us. Not long after the church was built, a grand boulevard was also constructed, running from just outside the door of the church all the way down the estate. It was called Belle Vue, after the Denison mansion itself, and this almost forgotten moment of history would become a matter of defining importance in 2022.

But it is a name that makes a different kind of sense as well. I often think about a conversation I had years ago with my friend Andrea, who was ordained a few years before I was, and, during the period of time covered by this book, was the chaplain at Trinity College in the University of Toronto, and also an honorary assistant priest at St. Stephen's. We were in a greasy spoon in the east end, talking about attitudes to wilderness, about the fear of wilderness our society has come to hold, and

I suggested that the wilderness and the inner city were the same, in some important respects – complex ecosystems that require constant attention to detail, constant awareness, the learning of the specific truths of *where you are*, in a way that small cities and suburbs do not demand. In the Bible, the wilderness, the desert (in Greek and Hebrew, one word covers both), is the place you go to have your defences stripped away. It is the place you go to be remade by God – like Jacob's children in their wandering, like Jesus in his time of testing. And we are a wilderness of our own kind, here.

Founded in 1858, the church burned to the ground in 1865 and was rebuilt. At least from that time onward, a setback was created, so that Bellevue Avenue no longer ran to the church door; there was a stretch of wooden sidewalk now, and a small open space that looks, in archival photographs and drawings, like a churchyard. A visitor around that time noted that, despite the Denison origins of the church, the congregation was overwhelmingly working-class and poor. The rebuilt St. Stephen's seems to have surfed from crisis to crisis, somehow never quite going under. There are records of discussions about its possible closure in 1912, and in 1925, and in 1958. And yet it also kept on changing, responding, reaching into the variable wilderness of its volatile place.

The rich, complex history of Kensington Market has been written about by many people more expert than me – how the Denison family, their fortunes declining, began to sell little packages of land to recent arrivals, ultimately allowing for the growth of what was first the 'Jewish market,' and then also the Portuguese Market, the Caribbean Market, the Latin American and African Market, a palimpsest of the history of immigration to Toronto; the little enclave's history as a home of anarchist politics from Emma Goldman onward, as the base of anti-racist activism and anti-fascist punk rock; the way the rundown firetrap of crowded buildings provided low-income housing for artists, myself among them, and how every year Ida Carnevale would light the new flame of the solstice at the corner of Augusta Avenue and Oxford Street and lead an ever-growing parade of puppets and cardboard horses in the most extraordinary neighbourhood ritual in Toronto, how the park filled up with drummers and fire spinners on summer nights. And St. Stephen's was always there, one way or another, the strange little church involved in every community twist and turn.

But there was probably no time more important than the decade from 1972 to 1982, when Cam Russell was the priest. Cam believed profoundly that the role of the parish church was to be there for everyone in the neighbourhood, for whatever they needed. And there were unemployed men, some of them unhoused, who needed sandwiches, and even more, needed someone to listen to their stories, so Cam and his wife, Shirley, started to offer both, and gradually it grew into Stop 103, named for the church's address at 103 Bellevue, and from there to the Stop Community Food Centre, which still operates, though in a different location, grounded in principles of food access and economic justice and mutual aid and respect. It was Cam who began to welcome the new Caribbean community into the church, and saw that the neighbourhood needed ESL classes, and daycare, and assistance in navigating the immigration system, so he worked with others to create St. Stephen's Community House, which has now developed into a major citywide multi-service agency called The Neighbourhood Group, or TNG, a group that will feature heavily in this story. TNG now has multiple buildings across the city, providing an extraordinary range of services. Within Kensington Market alone they offer day programming for seniors, a youth drop-in and art studio, newcomer services, a daycare, community mediation, a legal clinic, and more. TNG also runs, just around the corner from St. Stephen's, a drop-in, six days a week, for unhoused and marginally housed people, with on-site nurses, a doctor, counsellors, trustees, and an overdose prevention site, as well as a peer training program, which has provided many of their clients with employment and helped them to stabilize their lives. Cam attended their AGMs until the year he died, and the last time I saw him, very frail and ill by then, he was just coming back from lunch with their executive director. It was Cam Russell who made this little church, in so many ways, what it would continue to be, the church for all the Market, the place every-one could – and did – come.

For whatever it is worth, for all the years since the 1856 rebuild at least, there was a yard between the church and a wooden pedestrian walkway, which eventually became a concrete sidewalk. Houses were built down both sides of the street, with lawns reaching out over the space that had been the broad expanse of Belle Vue. Parish dinners and picnics happened in the churchyard. We don't know when the first people found overnight refuge there, but we know that hungry people were coming here for food at least from Cam Russell's time and probably long before, and that some of them were itinerant, unsheltered, and it would be surprising if no one lay down in that yard to sleep.

We know for certain that it was a place of shelter by the 1990s, because when I was sorting through parish papers to deposit them in the diocesan archives, I found a letter from that period, when Doctors Hospital had administrative offices in the church, and one of their administrators had written to the priest at the time, Kevin Flynn, to complain that too many homeless people were sleeping in the yard. (Kevin's response, also preserved, amounted to 'What kind of hospital even are you?')

When I first started talking to the bishops about going to St. Stephen's, I looked at the financial statements, which were reasonably catastrophic – but I also noticed that more than half of the parish's tiny income was being spent on their free community breakfast program. And when I went to talk to the long-time churchwarden, Leroy, a man I would come to admire more deeply than almost anyone I have ever met, he said to me, 'You know, I understand that if you come in as a new rector, you're going to have to make decisions, you're going to want to change things, there may be things you have to cut. But you need to understand that the community breakfasts are untouchable. That's the one thing we can't stop doing.'

The parish was as close to the end, at that point, as it ever got, under diocesan administration for a decade, massively in debt for some of that time, the subject of a controversial TVO documentary, and of neighbourhood organizing and gossip and constant speculation. For a while, there had been a FOR SALE sign in the yard, and although that was no longer there, my first contract was for just three months, because no one could be sure that it would survive any longer than that. And I was a kind of Hail Mary pass, the last chance, a new priest no one was sure what to do with, sent to an old parish no one was sure what to do with, in the hope that something good might happen, largely thanks to an area bishop who was at least as risk-seeking as I am myself.

I am not the person who should evaluate what happened, but I do know that we are still here. Tenuous, embattled, but still weirdly persistent, weirdly undefeated, this little outpost in the desert. When I was training for the priesthood, I read an essay by Rowan Williams calling on the Church to realize itself as

> a certain kind of space for human beings, a space that does not belong to any sub-section of the human race but – because it is first the space cleared by God – is understood as a space where humanity as such is welcome. It is not defended against anyone; it exists because of the defencelessness of God in the crucified Jesus. Those who occupy it are not charged with marking it out as a territory sharply defined over against territory that is the property of others; they are to sustain it as a welcoming place.

In many ways, everything I have done at St. Stephen's has been an attempt to realize this vision in one small actual place.

The Kensington Market area was already my neighbourhood – I lived in the middle of the Market for a while, though later to the south, by Alexandra Park. By the time I became the priest here, we had begun fighting rearguard actions against gentrification and the incursions of the forces of uncontrolled wealth in the Market, and over the years we had a few qualified victories – preventing a Walmart, and a giant nightclub called Liquor Donuts – but more losses, most of the raw food sellers going, Casa Acoreana closing, artists and low-income tenants driven out of the Chicken Lofts, the former chicken slaughter-house on Kensington Place, to make room for an illegal Airbnb. In fact, Airbnb started emptying out the Market as early as

2014, and I remember a few years of people calling the church in despair, saying, 'My landlord is taking down the door of my room and telling me it's an Airbnb now, what can I do?' And all I could do was tell them to call the legal clinic, but that never worked. A few tenants refused to be terrorized, and held their ground, but increasingly few. Once, just once, community activists managed to move quickly, in a multi-unit building, to help the tenants organize, and we beat back an eviction, and in 2020, in one of our few unqualified wins, the Kensington Market Community Land Trust was able to purchase that building and guarantee permanent stability for the people living there. But mostly it was eviction after eviction.

A few months after I started at St. Stephen's, Andrea and I had lunch with the sculptor Timothy Schmalz, who had recently had a lot of press coverage for a controversial statue of Jesus as a homeless person lying on a bench, a statue rejected by Roman Catholic cathedrals in New York and Toronto, but ultimately installed at Regis College, a Jesuit college within the University of Toronto (another cast of the same statue was eventually installed at the Vatican). He told us he had a plan for another statue that he'd long dreamed of installing at St. Stephen's: Jesus as a panhandler, sitting with one outstretched hand, and on that hand the wound of the crucifixion. We were nowhere close to being able to afford to install a full-size bronze, but Tim had a fibreglass cast, and he offered to let us have it outside the church for a while.

The neighbourhood response was dramatic. People immediately started leaving flowers and other offerings by the statue and spending long periods kneeling or sitting in front of it. One day, an Indigenous man named Winter came into my office to introduce me to a friend of his, someone he thought needed my counsel. 'You stay here and talk to Mother Maggie,' he said to her. 'I'll be outside with Jesus.'

We realized we had to try to raise the money for a permanent bronze. But just as we were starting on this intimidating task, one morning in November 2013, someone ran into my office shouting, 'They've stolen Jesus!' The fibreglass statue was gone. People in the area, some of whom had seen for the first time, in this statue, Jesus as one of themselves, were distraught, coming into the church crying. One neighbour phoned the *Toronto Star*, and, presumably because it was a slow news day, we ended up on the front page the next day.

By this time, I can only assume, the person who had taken the statue (I have always imagined that it was a student) was in a terrible position. And after an astonishingly symbolic three days, one of my volunteers found Jesus sitting on our back stairway, with a note attached reading, 'I'm sorry, it seemed like a good idea at the time.'

Perhaps it was, in an unintended way, a good idea after all, since the media attention made it possible for us to raise the money for a permanent bronze, which now sits at the northwest corner of the church, just beside the encampment. People have universally, from the beginning, called the statue Homeless Jesus, although technically Tim named it *Whatsoever You Do*, and it – or rather he, because everyone speaks about the statue as a person – should more properly be called *Panhandler Jesus*. I have tried to insist on calling him Panhandler Jesus, but ultimately I have given in. He has become our most clear visual identifier; we were 'the church that has Homeless Jesus' until we became 'the church with the encampment.' And he has watched over all the events of this book, a presence, a vision of solidarity and love.

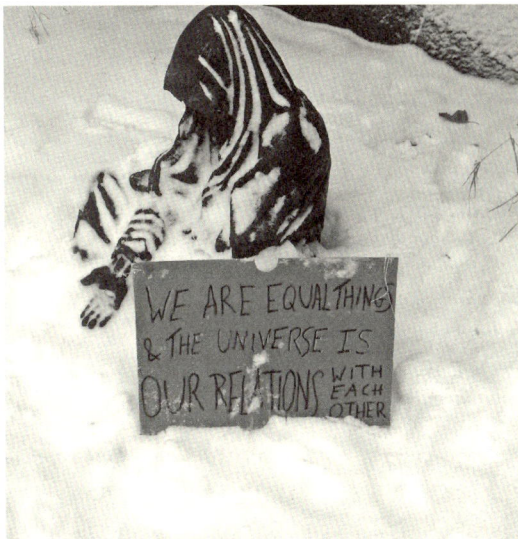

WE ARE EQUALTHINGS
& THE UNIVERSE IS
OUR RELATIONS WITH EACH OTHER

In January 2014, in a winter of extreme cold, the long campaign by activists for a warming centre at Metro Hall, an office tower that is the chief administrative site for the City of Toronto, finally bore fruit, but it was one of the most grudging municipal gestures possible, a large, drafty lobby with some chairs and a couple of boxes of granola bars, so Andrea and I brought in some food from the supermarket and were told we could only give it to people if we took it outside. And once we had spent the next two days arguing and lobbying to win the right to give away food inside the building, it seemed like we had to follow through, so for most of the rest of the winter we dragged our little bundle buggy full of towel-wrapped boxes of pizza pockets and trays of empanadas donated by one of the Market businesses into Metro Hall every night, until our relentless passive-aggressive shaming compelled the City, late in February, to start offering hot meals.

In May, I put down a load of topsoil in the yard at the southeast side of the church and created a tiny community garden space, in company with a frail elderly schizophrenic and a young homeless man recently out of prison, and someone who turned up out of nowhere to say that he needed some community service hours but WAS DEFINITELY TOTALLY COMMITTED TO US FOREVER and WOULD CERTAINLY NEVER LEAVE MY SIDE, a commitment that didn't last quite long enough for him to get his community service letter from me at the end of the day. And things went on like that for a few years, I suppose.

Then, on Canada Day in 2016, I arrived at the church to find it surrounded by police tape, and I had to be escorted into the building through the back door by police officers, because during the night there had been a double murder outside the unlicenced nightclub two doors down, and the whole block was being combed for forensic evidence. I started to think about this, about the number of bars within a few blocks, the lack of anywhere else to go at night, how hard it would be to find a safe space, and I phoned my risk-seeking bishop and said, 'I'm thinking of just leaving the church open all night on weekends to see what happens, how does that sound to you?' Unsurprisingly, it sounded good to him. And so, by a sort of accident, our Friday night drop-in was created.

It turned out there weren't a whole lot of people looking for safe space in the midst of the bar scene; but there were many, many people who had nowhere else to go. A lot of them were people who had been restricted from shelters, people with the deepest wounds, people who needed the lowest-barrier, least official space that there could be. And at St. Stephen's, a little group of semi-trained volunteers, with a vision of the church as an open space for all, and the body of Christ as every one of us, created, for a time, that space. It was utterly needed, and it was stupidly unsustainable, and for about a year and a half we rode that contradiction, and it nearly broke us all.

Perhaps it is enough to say that, the last time we stayed open all night, Chaz the Agent of Chaos, the young man who one summer day overturned our Homeless Jesus statue and crawled inside with a spray bottle of water to disarm the bomb he believed was concealed there, rode his bicycle through the middle of the church, howling in some strange kind of triumph, before returning to the bathroom and stripping off most of his clothes. Then, when dawn finally arrived, every toilet in the building backed up, and sewage began erupting up through the drain in the kitchen floor, and when I tried to make the breakfast volunteers stop preparing food, they insisted to me that everything was fine, and they would just wear boots and keep going, and meanwhile Chaz was desperately wielding a plunger in the janitor's closet, because he could hear someone screaming, imprisoned in the basement, and that was the only way they could be freed.

It took tears and accusations and meetings and many emails, but we closed at midnight after that. And if all that we established was that we are not in any meaningful way more sane than the people we are supposedly helping, that is in its own way an important piece of knowledge. Some of the regulars blamed Chaz the Agent of Chaos, who had also stuffed a plastic bicycle seat into a toilet to be a 'special filter,' who had also come running out of the bathroom with no pants and unwashed hands and systematically touched every food-handling surface, who had also turned up at a Saturday night church service and interrupted the proceedings for an hour, demanding that I tell him how to find a girlfriend, and then came back on Sunday morning and performed spontaneous interpretive dance for the congregation. The regulars weren't wholly wrong, but Chaz was in his own way only a symptom, only a part of the general storm.

'In the eyes of God, I'm no better and no worse than Chaz,' I said in one discussion, and one of our other nightly guests replied, 'I don't know. I think a *lot* of people are better than Chaz.'

'But I do believe,' said our saintly volunteer John, 'that if Chaz was the only person in the world, Jesus would still have died for him.'

This is how 2017 ended: there was a blizzard on Christmas Eve. And one of the people who came to our Christmas Eve Mass had nowhere else to go, and he had run out of his meds, and the pharmacies were all closed, so I agreed to sleep in the church that night so that he could also stay. In the morning, as we were cleaning up from breakfast, he thought he heard someone calling him a pedophile, and put his hand through the glass in the door of the foyer, cutting open a large vein, and my deacon Elizabeth bound it up with some gauze and took him to the hospital, while someone else cleaned up the blood on the church floor. And at the altar, during the service, I, exhausted, swung the incense burner straight into a chalice of wine and sent it right over, so my assistant and I were walking in a puddle of wine for the rest of the service, singing all the time because you don't stop singing.

Sacred infant, all divine, what a mighty love was thine, so to come from highest bliss, down to such a world as this.

For such a world as this is where we live.

Plague

This is not meant to be a story about COVID, except that the story of everyone who has lived through these years is about COVID somehow. It is about vulnerability and care, about people who were frightened and brave, and a time when, for just a little while, compassion was something that society's narrative understood.

I didn't see what was coming any earlier than anyone else who reads the news, and later than some. The first time I thought that this might be serious was when I heard of the purpose-built COVID hospital in China collapsing because it had been constructed so rapidly. It wasn't until COVID was cutting a swathe of illness and death through Italy that I started to expect it here. Some of my parishioners began wearing masks weeks before I did. My father-in-law died in a nursing home in British Columbia, maybe COVID before we had tests for COVID, and my husband was booking a flight to the funeral and suddenly there were no flights and no funeral, and I was as much caught off guard as everyone else.

But I will give myself credit for prescience in one thing. When I was summoned, along with hundreds of other workers in what we must call the 'homelessness sector,' to a Zoom meeting with Toronto Public Health, and Shelter, Support and Housing Administration, on March 11, 2020, to talk about plans for handling COVID-19 within the City's shelter system, I was the person who unmuted to ask what the City's plans were for people who slept outside and used the drop-in system, but didn't access City shelters. I got no answer, and sometimes I think that everything else that would unfold in our yard over the next years was implicit in that moment.

I believe that, at that time, the City's senior staff still thought that this question was about a small group of people. But every drop-in worker, and every front-line outreach person, knew about all the people throughout the city who were sleeping at night in Tim Hortons and McDonald's, or in the lobby of Toronto Western Hospital, or sleeping during the day in the public libraries and walking the streets all night, or moving between churches to sleep at the Out of the Cold overnights, or coming into the low-barrier warming centres when the sheltered corner of a building was too cold, the people with tents in the ravines, the people under the play structures in Bellevue Square Park, the people who were in the church every Friday night. I and others estimated the number at three to five thousand. Maybe that was accurate, at that time. It would become larger.

Two days after that meeting, the Out of the Cold network closed down, never to reopen again. Our guests sat in the drop-in, stunned by the news. 'But where will we sleep tonight?' one man asked. 'McDonald's,' his friend replied. At 10 p.m., just as I was getting ready to hand over to our late-shift volunteers, I received an email from the bishop, informing the Anglican clergy of Toronto that we were to suspend all church activities, effectively immediately, including all public worship services, with the single exception of 'ministries to the poor and vulnerable.' So I was in church that Sunday, at 5 a.m., along with my deacon Elizabeth, and a volunteer who showed up at the door in a World War II gas mask, handing out what we could put together for breakfast, little plastic baggies of bread slices with packets of peanut butter and jam by the time we got to the end of the line of people. When it was over, we went into the church, and Elizabeth livestreamed me on their phone, as Esther and I sang Mattins in the empty chancel.

And over the course of the next week, it all went away, every formal and informal support on which people had relied, all the Tims and the McDonald's and the libraries, all the heated lobbies, all the church overnights, nearly every drop-in across the city. For those first frantic weeks, we were one of only five drop-ins that continued to let people come inside. All the doors were closed. That Friday afternoon, I had to talk down a desperate, screaming man who had literally torn our back door from its hinges. Another of our regular guests sat in a chair sobbing and told me it was the first time in three days he'd been able to sit down, and that he was going to try to get himself hospitalized if he could, or arrested if necessary. We had just one box of masks, which I had purchased earlier in the day at a bizarrely inflated price, and we rationed them carefully between our volunteers. We didn't know how we would be able to buy enough bread, eggs, the staple goods now being restricted at groceries because of hoarders.

And yet it wasn't that new. We weren't entirely unprepared; there had been hepatitis and HIV and tuberculosis in the street population forever, we already knew about universal precautions, we already understood risk assessment. And it was all risk assessment for weeks and months, because my core of volunteers and I were never isolated, despite eliminating essentially all our social contacts to protect them, because my bubble was my immediate family and hundreds of homeless people, and every day in the back of my mind I planned how to isolate from my family if it came to that. Everywhere I went, I carried a letter from my bishop identifying me as an essential worker, permitted and required to go anywhere, as needed.

For more than a year, I would come back home from serving breakfast and celebrate Mass in front of a webcam in my tiny office, looking out the window, a red-winged hawk in the tree one Sunday, snow gathering on the fence when winter came.

We didn't understand COVID transmission very well – no one really did – and we spent a great and unnecessary amount of time wiping surfaces with alcohol over and over, and creating hot-room and shower protocols for coming home at night. But what we did understand is how you keep going, that you improvise, that you scramble fast, and that we need each other. A local brewery brought us a twenty-litre bucket of alcohol sanitizer. A neighbour fixed our door for free. When there was no bread in the stores, someone got a huge bag of flour from the now-closed restaurant where she had worked and started baking dozens of loaves at home every week.

We made that one box of masks stretch for weeks. Eventually we managed to buy one more, and some people made their own cloth masks. And then one day in early May there was a knock at the door, and a courier handed me box after box, sent by the City, filled with masks and face shields and gowns and hand sanitizer. I asked if he was sure that it wasn't for some other group with a similar name, and he said no, it was definitely for the church. It turned out that an amazing worker at the Toronto Drop-In Network had remembered us, and had made sure we, with our tiny shoestring operation, were included in the list of drop-ins to receive shipments of PPE.

Quickly – and a brilliant data visualization from the *Toronto Star* made it clear how quickly – the disease was socially directed; it moved from something randomly spread to something that existed among those who were poor, Black, low-wage workers who couldn't stay home, and people who had no homes in which to stay. I don't remember who it was who described this phase as 'rich people hiding while poor people brought them things,' but it is not untrue. And my community was, is, mostly poor or Black or both. The brother of my long-time altar guild stalwart died alone, in his apartment next door to hers. People died in shelters, from COVID, from toxic drugs.

On May 25, George Floyd died under the knee of a police officer in Minneapolis, and a brave teenage girl filmed the murder on her phone. Protests swept through the United States at the same time that the government of Ontario decided it was time for consumer activity to resume, so lines of hopeful shoppers stretched out along Bloor Street at the same time that stores were barricading their windows in case riots should suddenly break out on Bay.

'How to talk about theology,' I asked in a sermon that weekend:

> … when anyone who walked downtown yesterday walked past street after street of plywood, major retail centres all boarded up in a bizarre anticipation of a riot that never was, a disturbing symbol of this society's fear of the justified anger of Black activists and their anti-racist allies? How to talk about theology when, this

week, the president of the United States cleared the area around St. John's Church in D.C. with tear gas and flash-bang grenades, driving away a crowd which included the clergy, who had been handing out water and snacks to protesters, so that he could stand for seventeen seconds in front of a closed building holding a Bible upside-down, recalling nothing so much as the abomination of desolation described by Jesus in the gospels of Mark and Matthew?

How to go into the world in the name of the Trinity when our book, our faith, can be used in this way? When this grotesque tableau reminds us so forcibly that the church has been on both sides of this story, that Black people have found in the church a story of liberation which has carried them, a place of safety and community which has protected them, but also sometimes yet another zone of oppression, exclusion, and violence? That we still look every day at pictures of an inexplicably white Jesus, though one of the few things we can know as a historical certainty is that he was not that, was in fact a dark-skinned man murdered by the legal authorities of his time; that though the Episcopal and Anglican churches are trying to reckon with their history of racism, our complicity in colonialism, slavery, and brutality, our church still remains dominated by a mostly white leadership – including, in a small way, myself? What does the doctrine of the Trinity mean in this complicated context?

Everything, perhaps. Because if the doctrine means only one thing, it is this: we are all connected, and the life of one person is the life of all. We are made by the wind, by the breath and the voice, in the image and the likeness of God, and that image, and that likeness, are not single or isolated, but exist as a community of love. God is community, God is society, inherently, a society of mutual love and the grace which holds space for the others, of radical equality and interdependence, the society we are very much not, but always called to become. Even at the moment before creation, God was not alone, but was the dynamic movement of relationship, the creating intelligence of the word, the life-giving movement of the breath, and the great force of existence which calls all things forth and declares them all, all of them, every bit of this hurting world, to be good, to be very good, to be a world created in order to be beloved. We must not betray this vision. We must not betray this world.

❦

I enrolled myself as a rider for the People's Pantry, one of the mutual aid networks that sprang up in that strange season, and through the spring and summer I transported pans of casseroles and tubs of soup, cooked by another crew of volunteers, through streets nearly empty of traffic, riding my bike to Scarborough, East York, Eglinton and Scarlett, anywhere people had signed up to say that they needed food. Up the steep hill of Kingston Road in the late-afternoon heat and flying down again as dusk began to gather. To orphaned red-brick mid-rises in Leaside, or little houses in Mount Dennis, coming home along the Don Valley Trails, shaky from dehydration and low blood sugar. One of the volunteer cooks took a picture of me as I picked up a delivery from her, in my bike shorts and T-shirt, plastic gloves and surgical mask, pans of food in a cardboard box strapped onto the rack over the rear wheel. Bicycles of the apocalypse.

For just a short time, there was a focused attempt by governments to provide more housing, if only because housed people saw this as a means to protect themselves. At the start of the pandemic, as at no other time, when someone disappeared, it was at least as likely to be a good thing. Some people got into housing and stayed there. One of those people, to everyone's surprise, was Chaz the Agent of Chaos, who became a suddenly reformed character, devoted himself to the care of several little fluffy dogs, and signed up for the TNG Peer Training program. But as much of a relief as this was, it was not nearly enough, there were thousands of others, and there seemed to be more every day.

It was around this time that tents began to appear in the parks. Shelters were full, they were always full, and they weren't safe anyway, and some front-line agencies started handing out tents. We had a pleasant young couple tenting in the yard of the church for a while, but it wasn't, at that point, a preferred space – it was too small, too exposed to street traffic, too noisy. We didn't take special note of the tent; it wasn't that different from the handful of people who had always stayed in the yard. We didn't see it as the first moment of something that would come to define us.

Douglas, who had slept in the yard, without a tent, before the pandemic ever began, and kept on sleeping in the yard afterwards, was a much greater presence – he had been for years already, attending Sunday services regularly, as well as using the church as an address. One day, early on in the pandemic, someone let Douglas into the building in the morning – apparently he assured them I would be okay with it – and by the time I happened to go in and find him, he had built a small civilization of tables and chairs and odds and ends in the parish hall, which took most of a day to disassemble, while he tried to talk to me about his ex-girlfriend and how she would certainly get back together with him if he could just explain himself another time, Douglas being in this respect not greatly different from most other men. And one summer night, when I had to come in at 2 a.m. to secure the building after a door was left unlocked, Douglas followed me and the night cleaner around as we checked the doors, repeating, '*Excuse* me? *Excuse* me? Is *someone* going to make me a cup of coffee?' I would go out to the yard to let him use my cellphone to call his workers and tell them how useless they were, and we would make appointments for him to talk to me about all his ex-wives and how nothing had at any point been his fault.

As early as that spring and summer, I was part of difficult and confusing meetings between activists and City staff, trying to shape – or even identify – the City's response to the hugely increased numbers of people sleeping outside, sometimes in more visible tent communities. In April, the City had created an Encampment Working Group, which then became the Encampment Steering Committee, and was eventually replaced by the Encampment Office, a division of the Office of Emergency Management, entirely separate from Shelter Services or Streets to Homes (although it was brought under the Shelter Services umbrella eventually, late in 2023). Information about the Encampment Office was not available through a public search of City materials until several months after it was adopted into Shelter Services, more than two years after its formation. Lists of directors or staff did not exist for public access. We know that, at least for some time early on, it was headed by Jon Burnside, a former right-wing city councillor and former police officer. I had no idea how large a role the Encampment Office, in its various incarnations, would come to play in my life.

Two men set up a makeshift structure outside a closed building a few blocks south of the church, and the owner of the building wrote to me, because she didn't want to displace them – one of them was a frail, elderly man who had once worked for her father – but also wanted to be able to go ahead with planned renovations. So I spent a week phoning Streets to Homes every day, and waiting with the two men for hours for a visit, and when Streets to Homes finally sent an inexperienced and insensitive worker who stormed off in a temper about 'being disrespected' within the first ten minutes, I phoned more people, and went up the chain of authority far enough to get a more experienced worker sent out, and he found a decent shelter space for the two men and convinced them it was okay to go there. This was widely regarded as a miracle outcome, and led for a while to a perception that I had special and unique Streets to Homes powers. In September, one of the community police officers emailed me to ask if I, the parish priest, could somehow make Streets to Homes return the many phone calls from the police about people who wanted some kind of indoor space.

Out in the world from which I was increasingly distant, businesses opened, people ate on patios, businesses closed again sometimes. A street party outside my bedroom window went on for three summer nights, and included a bonfire, a sound system, and a novelty visit from a Mountie. We scrounged for food, handed out more and more meals. More people died.

From one of my sermons from October of that year:

Jesus does not say that we must love our neighbours as long as they also love us. He does not say that we must love our neighbours as long as they maintain some kind of basic standard of human decency. He doesn't even say that we must love our neighbours as long as they are not trying to kill us – and by this time in the gospel narrative, some of his neighbours are quite actively trying to kill him. We must love. We must love among the hate and the injustice, among the ruins, we must love those who do nothing to earn love. In pain, in fear, in grief, in terror and illness, we are called to reject the dark responses of the instinctual brain, and make that unnatural, essential turn toward love. Somehow, we must love them all. All the ideologues, all the terrorists, all the CEOs demanding the sacrifice of lives for economics, all the politicians taking advantage of tragedy, all the people on the internet spewing nonsense and hatred. We must love them all. We must desire their healing. We must pray for them too …

The story of the death of Moses, in today's first reading, has a number of odd features. Among them is the fact that Moses is described as dying alone in an unknown location, but also as being buried. Out of this contradiction arose the rather touching rabbinical story that, in fact, God buried the body of Moses personally. It is an expression of the same kind of intimacy we see in the incarnation. God, the unspeakable I AM, loves the world enough to have hands and to dig in the dirt, loves us enough to be with us in care and humility, now and at the hour of our death. And so we are cared for, in the work of God. Many of us have lost people in recent weeks. Some of us have lost people who died isolated and alone; and yet, they were not alone, never truly alone. It is still a frightening world and frightened world, but our safety is absolute in this. We must love one another, and die in any case, and we may die without entering our promised land, but we never die alone.

In December, Elizabeth and their partner got COVID, the first of our core group of volunteers to do so, probably not from the drop-in but because their partner worked in a warehouse. Elizabeth would recover fairly quickly. Their partner – thirty years old, strong, previously healthy – would never be entirely well again.

And then there were rumours, and there were tiny releases of information and suggestions that we should start creating lists of front-line staff, and one Friday night in mid-January, and once again thanks mostly to the Toronto Drop-In Network, I was one of the 'directors' who received a highly confidential email containing a link where my volunteers could sign up for a City-run vaccine clinic, created for shelter and drop-in staff, a clinic that would open that coming Monday.

Because our drop-in runs on Friday night, we were there and we were working, and most of us signed up for the first day of the clinic, although it was supposed to run for four weeks. And on January 18, I was among the first people in Toronto to receive a dose of the new Moderna vaccine. I remember looking at the sun in the high windows of the Metro

Toronto Convention Centre and thinking that this was a historic moment. It was less historic, I guess, in retrospect than it seemed at the time, as more and more variants emerged, as the vaccine proved only partially effective against them; but we forget, now, what it was like, how many people were dying, that on the Friday when we got that link, I felt a heavy cloud of fear, to which I'd become so accustomed that I hardly noticed it any more, lift from my shoulders.

On that first day, the link was leaked (apparently by a low-level employee at Public Health), and several hundred ineligible people showed up and were vaccinated, and by day two everyone coming had to present letters attesting to their identity and their work. At the end of the second day, the province, saying they were concerned about vaccine supply, shut down the clinic. Those of us who'd already attended were told that we would definitely get our second shots somehow but no one was sure how. Those who had registered for the later dates were simply told that they would have to wait, that there would be something for them at some point, no one knew when. Which is also what it's like to work in this sector, I suppose.

In between my first shot and my second, I developed acute appendicitis, lay in the emergency department at Toronto Western Hospital on an antibiotic drip for more than twenty-four hours waiting for an operating room to be free, had my appendix removed, was sent quickly home. When I went in for my second shot, the day after I had been released, it was already becoming clear that something wasn't quite right, and the day after that I was readmitted, vomiting and crying and in the worst pain I have ever known, with an intestinal obstruction, apparently a common, though occasionally life-threatening, surgical complication. Some of the staff wheeling my stretcher from place to place in the hospital wore buttons reading, 'I got my COVID vaccine!' along with their rainbow lanyards and colourful caps. We felt like members of a secret society together. For a while the first night, I had to be parked in the psychiatric ER because there was no room anywhere else, and after the nasogastric tube started to draw off the fluid and I came out of a morphine haze, I kept thinking that I needed to get out of bed and intervene in things.

The next morning I was wheeled to a private room in a corner of the general ward. I realized, as they took me in, that the room next door was where I had sat for days, a few years back, with a man who was dying. I took part in an Ash Wednesday service on Zoom from my bed, my surgical mask covering the sight of the nasogastric tube. I could look out the window to tents in Alexandra Park, where I had delivered sandwiches and packaged salads.

I watched the seagulls over the distant sliver of lake, watched the sun as it set. I lay in the bed for three more days, watching the lake and the birds, and in a strange way it was one of the sweetest times of my life, alone in a small bed in a white room, with warm blankets and no expectations. On Friday night, the nasogastric tube was removed, and I was allowed to sip water, and it tasted like the most wonderful fluid in the world. On Saturday, I was taken off the IV drip, and allowed to eat a small container of honey yogurt.

That night, a woman came into the room next door from one of the tents, and I could hear her crying most of the night, negotiating with a doctor, who sounded very young, explaining to him that she knew what her maintenance dose of fentanyl was, what she needed, and he was afraid that he would kill her if he gave her that much, and the worlds collided on and on through the darkness, and finally she ran away from the hospital and didn't come back.

On Sunday, I led the Zoom service from the 'family room' on the ward, and then I went home, still on a soft diet and walking gingerly, and when I walked through the Market, I was surrounded by my street friends wanting to be sure I was okay.

And maybe this is a dividing line of sorts, into a world of different plagues, multiple, complex, a world increasingly believing it had to get back to normal, as if normal had been good, as if it were something we should want to get back to. There was a window, just a little window in time, when it had seemed that the pandemic might actually help us to imagine a new world (and, according to census data, in 2020 the average income in Kensington/Chinatown actually rose, entirely because of improvements in the economic condition of those in the lowest-income bracket). But it was always an illusion, and the forces of capital surged back instantly, and COVID became, instead, one of a crowd of factors pushing wealth toward the wealthy, and breaking even further those already broken. And the casualties of the surge were cast out, into the streets, into the parks, and finally right up to the churchyard.

❦

When some of the City parks first began to fill with tents in 2020, many people couldn't understand what was happening, couldn't see it as anything other than mischief. More specifically, John Tory, the mayor at the time, seems to have been wholly unable to imagine that anyone would live in a tent for any reason other than to make a political point, or to cause personal irritation to John Tory himself.

It is true, of course, that encampment is a well-established protest tactic. The Greenham Common Women's Peace Camp, set up to protest the presence of nuclear weapons at the U.K.'s Royal Air Force Base at Greenham Common, lasted for nearly twenty years and was a formative experience for many hundreds of British women. During the Gulf War of 1991, I was part of a rather sad little peace camp outside the provincial legislature, involving a dozen young anarchists sitting in mud for three weeks, after which everyone came over to the house where I was then living and failed to leave for some time. As I am writing this, encampments have been set up on university and college campuses around the world in solidarity with Palestine, and some of those encampments have been violently cleared.

Protest encampments and survival encampments are distinct and different phenomena – and yet there can be grey areas. Occupy Toronto set up in St. James Park in Toronto as a protest camp, but over the first few weeks, people without homes began to realize that this was a place of community and support, not to mention a place where hot meals were regularly provided, and some came and joined the protesters, pushing the young activists into relationships they had not expected with some of the victims of capitalism, forcing them to confront mental illness and addiction, pressing at the borders of their own understandings of what community could be. And while the encampments at Trinity Bellwoods and Alexandra Park and Lamport Stadium were unquestionably survival encampments, set up and inhabited by people who had no other decent choice, over the course of time they began, Trinity Bellwoods Park especially, to adopt some of the visual iconography of protest camps, especially as the City began to exert more pressure on them to move out.

In every case, encampment makes visible what has been hidden, forces afflicted bodies into the public eye. For protest encampments, that making visible is the aim, the only real purpose; for survival encampments, it is a side effect. But the discomfort caused to the comfortable is not wholly different.

So perhaps John Tory's insistence that people were living in the parks 'to make a point' was, at least partly, a mistake in good faith, though if it was, it was a stunningly naive mistake, and one that Tory clung to in the face of all evidence to the contrary.

And in the late spring of 2021, the hammer came down. The Office of Emergency Management took over the encampment file in May, and the clearings started almost immediately.

Just as encampments had been around for years, clearings had taken place for years. The ravines were usually left alone, but the camps under the Gardiner Expressway and the Bathurst bridge and others came and went, and the going was rarely voluntary. These large park encampments, though, were immensely more visible, and because of this, had acquired more allies.

It began at the Lamport Stadium in Parkdale, with a clearing that didn't happen. A friend texted me and asked me to come, hoping my de-escalation skills might come in useful. In fact, what ended up coming in useful was my first aid training, as, within the first half-hour, a young woman, trying to get from one side of the stadium to the other in too much of a hurry, came off her bike and hit the ground without a helmet. For the rest of the afternoon I ended up sitting with her, as she regained consciousness but in a state of confusion, waiting for the ambulance to arrive, trying to get her phone so I could call her girlfriend, making arrangements with others to take her bike to a safe place, and finally loading myself and my own bike into the ambulance with her to accompany her to Toronto Western. So

I missed the protests, the police horses, the arrests, missed the dismantling of a few tents and the withdrawal of the City workers in frustration.

Then on June 21, 2021, before dawn, something resembling a secret military operation began to gather in Trinity Bellwoods Park. People in the quiet leafy neighbourhood stared out their windows in astonishment. Streets were closed off, helicopters hovered overhead, there were lines of trucks full of police horses, ranks of riot squad officers, private security guards. I slipped into the north encampment as a massive security fence was being put up around it, getting in, I think, because while the police know how to deal with opposition, they are taken quite off guard by people who just quietly ignore them. We sat in the north encampment for a few hours, while residents packed up their tents and had discussions about where they might go, and one man danced in front of the line of riot police, and another rode past outside the fence on his bike, over and over, portable speakers blasting the Imperial Stormtrooper theme from *Star Wars*. Friends and I ended up helping to pack the tent of a young couple who had nowhere to go, and someone loaded their belongings into a car and drove them to the church, where they became the second couple to tent in the yard.

And then the riot squad started to advance, beating their sticks on their shields as they do, and shouting, bizarrely, 'WATCH YOUR STEP! BE CAREFUL! DON'T SLIP AND FALL! WATCH YOUR STEP!' Somewhere there is a photo of me, looking alone, although I wasn't, walking very, very slowly backwards, in front of this wave of official concern for my balance and overall wellness.

When all the residents of the north encampment had dispersed in the face of the riot squad, those of us who were there as supporters moved to the south encampment, outside the fence this time, though others had come inside there earlier on. And it was a strange afternoon that swung between a picnic sort of atmosphere with old friends, and sudden police surges into the crowd. We would be standing and chatting, and suddenly there would be screaming, and I would be once again kneeling on the ground washing someone's eyes clear of pepper spray. Sometimes protesters would jump onto the fence. Sometimes police horses would push into the crowd and knock people down. There were a few arrests, a couple of criminal charges. In the end, perhaps twenty to thirty people who had been living in the park that morning were chased away, at a total cost of over $400,000, according to a report later released by the City itself.

The young couple lived in our yard for a few days, but again found it too noisy, too exposed. One of them had relatives in Peterborough, and they managed to make contact and get on a bus to stay there for a while.

At Alexandra Park, up the street from my house, the residents requested that only a few trusted friends be there to help them when they were cleared out, and even so nine people were arrested, including a Canadian Press photographer. The day in July that the City moved on Lamport for the second time, I was dealing with an allergic reaction to an antibiotic (my body and its eccentric misadventures becoming more of a theme here than I might have thought), so I wasn't there, and I only know what anyone knows who has seen the news reports – that it was chaos, that protesters were injured, that twenty-six people were arrested, and that press photographs travelled around the world showing officers forcing protesters to the ground and wielding batons against them.

Two other big encampments were different. In Dufferin Grove Park, for whatever combination of reasons, the City invested the time and the money to move people out slowly and carefully, and to provide real housing alternatives. But the housing supply was exhausted after that, and the 'Dufferin Grove model' proved, for obvious reasons, impossible to replicate without that supply – even, eventually, in Dufferin Grove itself, when tents returned in 2024.

Moss Park, meanwhile, was the largest encampment in the city, the most organized, the most politically connected, and we held our breath to see what would happen there, fearing it would be even worse than Lamport. But the City chose not to move against Moss Park, and it remained, and it remains.

Trinity Bellwoods and Lamport and Alexandra were fenced. A few of us from the church came down to Alexandra Park, where we had held outdoor services in the past, and I celebrated Mass against the fence, while private security guards within the enclosure stared at us curiously.

The tents moved, instead, into the smaller parks: Bellevue Square and Sonya's Park and Randy Padmore Park in my immediate neighbourhood, Grange Park not far away. I found myself in a new role now, talking to neighbours and friends who had not anticipated the tides of affliction washing up onto their streets, who didn't understand, who were afraid, afraid of the woman who screamed all the time, of the angry tattooed men with big dogs on bits of string, of the emergency vehicles at night, of this edge of dystopia in a place where it was not expected. They didn't want to be cruel. They wanted to be like Dufferin Grove. But the housing was running out. Our then city councillor, Mike Layton, found a grant that allowed The Neighbourhood Group to hire encampment outreach peer workers, including one of my parishioners, Andrew, who would work for TNG from 2021 to 2023, and also develop into the church's most important volunteer encampment worker. But there was less and less to offer, nowhere for people to go.

Seasons move, suddenly it was winter. I sat on the floor of the church one night with a man in alcohol withdrawal, waiting for an ambulance, and it was one of the most peaceful times I had had for weeks. When the ambulance finally arrived, a huge Black paramedic named Nero lifted the man tenderly, helped him onto a stretcher, took him to a place of care. This man – funny, cynical, wounded – would be dead within a year, but he lived through that night.

Meanwhile Douglas, who was in his seventies and diabetic, was increasingly ill, and ended nearly every drop-in night lying in his own urine because he couldn't make it to the bathroom in time. We called ambulances for him and he refused to go with them; one night Andrew and I stood over him in a doorway across the street from the church as he lay, gradually being covered with snow, and the paramedics couldn't persuade him to go with them, because he was so sure – based on real past experience – that he would be formed and held against his will. Finally, one night, he couldn't stand up, and he agreed to let the ambulance take him to a hospital. He was in hospital for four days, and I was on the phone with the hospital social worker, trying to develop a discharge plan, when he turned up, shaking and barely mobile, at our front door, having been discharged to the church address without the social worker's knowledge. I called Andrew, and he pulled every personal string he had to pull, and we managed to grab one of the rare, precious shelter-hotel rooms, and somehow or other I persuaded Douglas to go.

We raced there in a car driven by one of my volunteers, and I got him checked in, and it seemed like a miracle. And he would leave the hotel eventually, as we always knew he would, and come back to sleep on the steps of the church, but it would be spring by then, and he would have survived the winter.

A friend of mine talks about his days on a suicide hotline, how, when you do that work, 'alive at sunrise' is the win. Sometimes we aim at more than a single sunrise. But it is the same, finally – every day is a victory, every week that death is held off is the win, this is what we do.

❦

I began one spring day trying to help the police identify a dead man in a doorway at Dundas and Kensington. Another day, someone was dead in Bellevue Square Park, an overdose, no one there close enough with naloxone, and his body lay on the grass for hours before the paramedics took him away. Sometimes when I was cycling to work in the morning, I saw City crews in Randy Padmore Park, ripping up tents with knives. Volunteers going down with COVID, in and out of isolation. I had always thought I might grow up to live in a dystopian future, but somehow I had imagined it being more exciting than it turned out to be.

I have talked about encampments as a solution of necessity, and they are that. But there are other things I need to explain. And the most important of these is that encampments can also be spaces of grace; that encampments, in a time of great affliction, can be home to creativity and community, healing and mutual support. I need to tell you that this, more than anything else, is what I began to learn in the summer of 2022, and after.

Douglas was still sleeping on our steps. Syed moved into the alcove where Dennis had been sleeping. And, as Grange and Bellevue Square were gradually emptied, a few tents started to appear again in the churchyard. It was still a noisy, exposed location, even worse now, in the middle of roadworks as the sewer lines were replaced and the street rebuilt, and then the streetcar tracks on College Street were being renovated, construction that seemed like it would go on forever. But there was nowhere else to go. This time, the tents would not go away, and more would come, and somehow, without our even intending it, we would end up as the face of encampment life in Toronto.

❦

The encampment grew rapidly, that first spring and summer of 2022. Robin and Bryan were probably the first to set up tents, while others slept unsheltered on the steps or in the yard. More soon followed, as enforcement in other nearby parks became more aggressive. I came back from a somewhat ill-fated trip to Prince Edward Island – during which I had gone through both food poisoning and an allergic reaction to a wasp sting, my daughter had fallen off her bicycle at speed on a rough road going downhill and acquired a permanent scar on her chin, and my husband had been exhausted, irritable, and inexplicably confused – to discover that the three or four tents that had been there when I left had increased to nearly a dozen, and there was no longer any part of the lawn without an occupant.

At that early point, it had an exuberant visual quality, with flags and banners suspended from the trees, and artistic installations being constructed and reconstructed every day along

the edges of the laneways, on discarded side tables and decorated trays, assemblages of flowers and broken furniture, rocks and candles and pieces of coloured glass. This creative energy would become the first casualty of the City's incursions, beginning late in the fall, as policy insisted that people should be allowed to have, at most, survival dwellings and no more than that, but for a while it was an oddly beautiful chaos through which I walked each day.

All kinds of people live in encampments, and each encampment takes on its own character. Ours was quickly known for a low level of violence, and a minimal presence of drug-dealing, although I know that some other encampments have had serious problems, that there have been guns and human trafficking sometimes. We watched for any signs that there were issues building, but they did not substantially happen; the worst act of violence on the site involved a penknife, and our residents were involved in the drug trade mainly as small purchasers. Perhaps it was partly because we had people regularly around, working in the church and nearby, who already had some credibility, who did intervene to stop some behaviours, and perhaps also because some of the earliest people to move in had a pre-existing relationship with the church and a high degree of respect for it. But, on the other hand, we have always had a population uncommonly fragile – 'high-need' in the jargon of the sector – people with service restrictions of many kinds, who wept on the steps of the church for reasons obscure to others, people whose obstacles to moving indoors were complex.

Mental illness, broadly understood, is practically a universal human experience, and if someone were not depressed or anxious before ending up on the street, it is pretty much guaranteed that they would be after. But what people usually mean, when they say mental illness, is schizophrenia. According to StatsCan, in 2016 about one in one hundred Canadians over the age of ten was living with diagnosed schizophrenia, so it is not really so rare, but it is one of several illnesses that can, sometimes, be a trigger factor for homelessness, and can certainly be made much worse by the conditions of homelessness. A significant proportion of people on the street who live with schizophrenia are aware of their diagnosis, and will be open about it with those they trust, and are often receiving treatment, but the fact is that we don't have very effective treatments, especially for those who have lived with the condition for a long time.

It's a condition greatly feared by those who haven't spent much time with it, but it is really best defined as a radically different way of perceiving the world. Things that for some people may be perceived as a subjective inner monologue may be perceived by others as an objective external voice. Things that may seem like random coincidental occurrences to some people may seem to others a complex pattern filled with meaning, sometimes beautiful, sometimes sinister. A flicker of light or shadow may be a solid object charged with intense, perhaps terrifying, significance. Thought may be rapid, hyperassociative, linking syllable to syllable in fractal patterns.

Some cultures, and some clinicians in this culture, have looked for other ways to manage this, have tried not to extinguish the voices but to help people build better relationships with them, to construct lives that include difference, acknowledge that medication may help but will never be enough. Acknowledge that the inner pit of confusion and hunger and despair, the desperate quest to make meaning of the random cascade of events, is simply human; it is only what we do with it that changes.

People who've been identified as 'presenting with mental health issues' (sometimes, ironically, abbreviated to 'presenting with mental health') have included Douglas and Isaac, grey-haired men who were once young and bright and on the verge of a shimmering world, who after decades on the street can be sometimes overwhelmed with grief and rage at what their lives have become. Isaac is a man of great gentleness, blessed for some years with a doctor who cared about him, and a room in a supportive boarding house, writing treatises about time travel, scrawling truly terrible dad jokes on scrap paper as what he calls his art, sometimes bringing his meds to the church so I can bless them, always willing to give the person beside him half of his sandwich or his chocolate bar or his spare change, sometimes needing a safe place where he can just scream until the sorrow of all that he has lost recedes. Douglas was clenched and suspicious, much of his character defined by incarceration in the Oak Ridges forensic psychiatric facility at a time when their therapeutic model was best described as torture, an experience acknowledged in the compensation paid to survivors. Convinced that teenage girls on the street were calling him a bad man, collecting 'letters of reference' from all and sundry, obsessed with his ex-wives and the girlfriend whom he could not admit had died of cancer, with whom he was still determined to reconcile.

Or the young man who explained that he needed to play loud music throughout the church service in order to drown out the voices, and was eventually more or less persuaded that a quieter conversation with the deacon might work. Or Bryan from Newfoundland, a voracious if indiscriminate reader, whose sudden outbursts of panic and rage are more likely to turn into self-harm than danger to others, Bryan who has bled onto our floors and at our front door, whose wounds I have so often washed. Or the other young man who played the piano and hung mystic symbols on the walls, and somehow turned up in the middle of a Lent procession with a lit candle, dancing down the aisle with it, enchanted – and who later died in police custody, reportedly a suicide, a story his family does not believe. Or the woman the community police call the Artist, one of our long-term encampment residents, combing the garbage cans of the Annex for her materials, her collages of magazine photos and safety pins on wood, living in multiple dimensions, who told someone once that I was Queen Elizabeth and she herself was Queen Victoria, so we were cousins really, whose veins are the branches of a tree, whose gentle mind roams infinite worlds.

Or Robin – Robin who was one of the first to set up a tent in the yard, after a decade bouncing from hospital to jail to street corners and doorways; who, when they first came to our yard, could communicate only by screaming. They would fly in the door, a storm of tattered clothing and loose hair, and pour a whole carton of milk onto the floor, or grab a full bowl of chocolate and run. But they stayed in the encampment. And a couple of people in the other tents started to look out for them, especially Jeff, our more or less mayor; Jeff and some others started to comfort them when they were distressed, visited their tent for tea, took them into other tents when their own collapsed. A remarkable caseworker from The Neighbourhood Group visited them regularly. There was less screaming. Mostly, still, all that most people heard from Robin's tent was demands that everyone go away. But one day, when City crews were all over the encampment seizing things and clearing walkways, the worker and I knelt by their tent, and inside it Robin wept quietly, and whispered to us that they had to stay here because they were protecting the earth and the grass.

And we promised them that they could protect the earth and the grass, and that no one would make them move, and we held off the City workers and kept that promise. And the week after that, when they were allowed to remain, they were calmer, and the week after that still better. They began, of their own volition, to take their meds again, and finally, months and years into their stay with us, they became the sweetest and truest presence in the whole community, not always stable, fragile as eggshell still, but smart, articulate, connected. Some of the other encampment residents complain that they feed the Market rats and try to train them as their pets, but everyone looks out for them.

'I feel safe here,' they said, this person who had once barely spoken single words. 'I think the church really cares about me. I put up some coloured plastic in my tent so it looks like stained glass; I think I'm becoming an Anglican, in a way, living here.' And another day, 'I'm so lucky, you know, to be able to live out here. To experience all the different weather, and see all the animals and the plants, and feel the wind and the rain. I'm just a really lucky person.'

❦

And yes, there are drugs as well. And alcohol, of course, that accessible, legal, nearly omnipresent short-term strategy. People are looking for ways to cope, ways to keep the trauma responses down, perhaps to quiet the voices, or to try to moderate cascading, terrifying moods. Or ways to sleep at night. Or ways to stay awake at night, so they won't be robbed or raped. There are reasons, and they are not foolish reasons.

Not so much for Douglas or Isaac, who had lively histories with LSD, but gradually gave up almost everything except some pot or an occasional beer. But for most people there is cheap whisky or mouthwash, there are prescription drugs like Ritalin, given out easily and in quantity; and there is also fentanyl, and there is crystal meth, those deeply mythologized substances, treated sometimes in the media as if merely passing them in the street will kill or ruin you instantly.

One of the recurring facts of homelessness is the lack of privacy – complaints about public drug use are really complaints that people have nowhere private to be, and especially nowhere private that they can use with friends, which everyone knows is safer. I am far happier about people using in the yard, where I and others can see them, than the back stairwell, which is hidden; one of my worst ongoing fears from the time I arrived was finding someone dead in the stairwell someday.

I have come to realize that there are people, housed and relatively safe, for whom visible drug use is, in itself, terrifying, people who experience seeing drug use by others as harm. I cannot deny their feelings; the feelings are real, their pain is real, although that does not necessarily mean that there is any actual threat. Some parents strongly believe that if children see adults using drugs, they are more likely to experiment themselves. There's no point in my saying that my sister and I are among the relatively few children of the educated middle class who were, thanks the work our parents did in the prisons, exposed to the realities of drug use at an early age, and responded by living adult lives of intimidating purity and abstinence; nor that their children are inevitably going to encounter drugs in high school, regardless of what they do or do not walk past on their way to kindergarten.

There are, frankly, few people who are less dangerous to others than a habitual user of opiates only – I think of Tyler, a sweet broken soul, sleeping on the floor of the parish hall, cradling a box of pancake mix, a few months before he overdosed and died. Crystal meth is different, yes, the euphoria swinging rapidly into mania, often into psychotic states that can take a long time to recede, if they ever do. But finally, it is only human beings trying to survive a flood of suffering. And none of us, when we are in that flood, make perfect decisions, but only the decisions we can.

One of the things that strikes me most about attitudes toward the encampment is the really deep conviction, on the part of housed people, that the encampment residents are somehow getting away with something, that they are on a kind of permanent fun vacation while everyone else is going to work and behaving nicely. People have talked about 'self-indulgence,' about 'entitlement.' It says something, I suppose, about just how miserable many middle-class people secretly are, that they imagine people living in tents in the freezing rain are somehow, and unfairly, having too much fun. But we are taught to think about street drugs that way. We are not taught that they may be an adaptive strategy to extreme suffering, which can make rational sense in the moment. We are not taught that they may be, at least sometimes, the last-ditch attempt, in the midst of affliction, to make it alive to sunrise.

❦

Beyond what we are taught about drugs, though, beyond what we are taught about psychosis, we are taught, most deeply and most consistently, not to be fragile. Not to be weak, or needy, or breakable. We are taught to despise fragility. To shun the people who embody it: the very old, the very young, the disabled.

One summer day, a man sat down on the steps of the church. At some point not long before that, he had injected opiates. And as he was sitting there, he suddenly went down, flat onto the street. Jeff's dog, which had learned to detect ODs, began to bark, and indicate toward the steps. People came running from the encampment, and by the time I heard the noise and opened the door, someone was doing chest compressions, someone else was administering naloxone. When the ambulance came, the man was already back. The encampment, with which he had no connection, of which he was perhaps completely unaware, had saved his life. It is the broken people who will run, over and over, to save strangers, when everyone else is too afraid.

The world is ill, and the world is fragile. But some people in the world can pretend that they are well. This pretence, on which many people base their identities, is so thin, so threatened by reality, that they must fight constantly to defend it, and fight against anyone who might make them think that it is not true. In the end, more than anything else, it is this, I believe, that drives the complaining neighbours, drives the City bureaucrats when they are brutal or callous, drives the violence that housed people can bring against the unhoused, drives the anger and the fear.

Needles won't really jump from the street and jab you through your clothes. The unconscious person on the corner will not suddenly leap up and assault you. The weeping woman with a badly fitting Marilyn wig will not take your job away. The true, terrible threat is that, if you just once let those people get too close, you might learn that, underneath it all, we actually are the same. Poor bare forked animals in King Lear's storm, in a world that is always ending.

This is a different kind of fragility, the fragility of the people who live in the land of the well, but who know, on some unadmitted level, that no one has permanent residency there.

I have never been much more than a tourist in the land of the well. And probably I should have been more patient, and I should have been more understanding. But the land of affliction is, one way and another, my home.

Disappearance

I want to take you back in time now, to 2018, not long after our ill-fated overnight program closed, not long after the Christmas Eve blizzard. People were coming to the church every Friday, for dinner and conversation and a few hours of rest, but only a handful slept in the yard, and those people only intermittently.

It's easy, and common, to talk about people without shelter as vulnerable people. We are all vulnerable people, really; we are all captives, as John Donne says, to 'war, dearth, age, agues, tyrannies, despair, law, chance'; all exposed to illness and failure and finally death, although some of us can run from that knowledge. But *vulnerable* is just a word, and what it means at the extremes can be hard sometimes to imagine. Things happened in 2018, some of them very public, some of them private; things that can, I think, tell us something both about the vulnerability of simply being human, and the particular, intense vulnerability of those who have been moved to the margins, who have been made invisible.

> *And I who am here dissembled*
> *Proffer my deeds to oblivion, and my love*
> *To the posterity of the desert and the fruit of the gourd.*
> – T. S. Eliot

Part of what makes front-line work so hard is the way that people disappear, the way that we don't see them for weeks and don't know what's happened, and maybe we hear after a long time that they have been in prison or that they've died, or maybe they vanish and we will never know. We can hope they've gone back to the rez, hope they've found family somewhere, but we know this is only hope.

And if you are a person who incarnates a certain kind of evil, you can take advantage of this. You can know that there will be people who may be missed, may be very much missed but will not be searched out.

In the summer of 2017, I had cycled up Toronto's Don Valley Trail, about once a week, past MISSING posters with a photograph of Andrew Kinsman. The police were still saying, then, that there was no serial killer in the Gay Village. That all those men who had disappeared, most of them so similar in appearance – bearded, brown-skinned – had maybe just gone away somewhere. Because they were the people who no one with power seeks. One of the missing men, Selim Esen, was in a peer support group at TNG, just around the corner from the church. He was fairly new to Canada, struggling a bit, no family here, relationship problems. He had been missing for over a year. His friends had done what they could, and yet nothing happened.

But Andrew Kinsman was different. He was white, middle-class, a community organizer. He had friends who were confident, connected, and relentless, who did far more than put up those posters in the ravine. Friends who knew, as so many people did, that this could not be just a series of coincidences. There was a serial killer in the Village, a systematic predator. Andrew's friends fought long enough and hard enough that the entrenched homophobia of the Toronto Police Service started to bend, and his case began to matter; even the others began, at last, to matter.

Andrew Kinsman, even dead, broke the silence.

The official denial didn't really shatter until one day in January 2018. It was very cold that day. I moved out of my office because it was too cold to work in there. I was at my computer in a side room with a space heater, sitting on the floor because that was the only way I could plug in my laptop, and that was where I watched the press conference. Someone had been arrested, someone who had killed Andrew Kinsman and Selim Esen. And others. There would be more charges, the police said.

Later on, I, like everyone else, would learn about what had just happened: the simultaneous lightning raids on several properties that had been planned for weeks, moved suddenly ahead in time when the suspected killer was seen bringing a young man into his apartment. We would learn how, during one of the raids, at a house in Leaside, a police dog fixed on a large planter and refused to leave it, though the soil was frozen and it seemed impossible that he could catch any scent. The planter was taken to an indoor location to thaw. In the soil, the investigators found what reports would always call 'human remains.'

More cadaver dogs came to the leafy, comfortable neighbourhoods of Leaside and Rosedale, working their way through frozen gardens.

Eleven days later, the police released more names. Majeed Kayhan's was expected, one of the men from the original investigation, which had come to nothing. Soroush Mahmudi was a troubling surprise, someone not named in any previous investigations, a suggestion there could be many more to come. But then there was the third man, whose image I recognized immediately. Dean Lisowick, though I had never known his last name. The kid – not such a kid, really, in his forties, but he had seemed so young, so vulnerable – who panhandled outside the 7-Eleven. Who'd lived in and out of the Scott Mission just up the street. The organist at my church told me he knew the other missing men, more or less, from seeing them around the community, but Dean was the one he talked to regularly, out on the street corner, the one he bought food for. Dean was the one I'd given toast and coffee at the church breakfasts.

Bryan, the volatile Newfoundlander who carried thick books wherever he went, was living on the streets near the church then, and was in nearly every day, reading in a corner, sometimes in a Superman costume. When the news broke, he came to us weeping. 'He was my buddy,' he said. 'He was my *boy.*' But no one could recall exactly when they saw him last.

We have all tried, since then, to reconstruct memories of the last time someone saw Dean. No one is sure. No one will ever be sure exactly when Dean was taken. Because he belonged to the group of those who may disappear, who have no community close enough around them to be certain they are gone. If there had been encampments in the middle of the city then, if he had found his way into one of them, someone would have noticed more quickly, might have made inquiries. It might not have changed anything else – though perhaps it could have. But it would have meant, at the very least, that his going was marked. That we would have known when he had disappeared.

And he said, Mortal, can these bones live? And I said, Oh Lord, thou knowest.

The phone call from the detective came very early in the morning one day in February; I talked to him while I was lying under the duvet in my cold bedroom. 'We think this man was preying on the homeless community,' he said. 'And we don't have the trust of that community. So we're calling people like you, people who do. We think you could be a valuable asset.' (*Valuable asset*, a phrase like *human remains*, a phrase you would never hear in ordinary speech.) 'Also,' he said, 'we've recovered some photographs from his computer, and we can't identify all the people in those photographs. We're reluctant to ask you to look at them. But at some point, we may have to ask you.'

In the end I was not a very valuable asset. But I talked to people at the drop-in, asked them about friends who hadn't been around for a while, asked if there was anyone they were worried about, and took descriptions to compare against police records. The police sent me only one photograph, and it had clearly been edited. It was disturbing only to the extent that it showed a man obviously dead, his face bruised and discoloured. In my earlier life as a human rights activist, I had seen secret, graphic photographs of Indonesian military torture, so this carefully cropped picture was not difficult to look at. Later, reports from journalists would describe some of the things that did not appear in this image: the killer's bizarre habit of dressing his victims in a fur coat after death, posing them with props, playing with them like giant dolls before cutting them into pieces. None of that was visible in that photo. And I could not identify the man.

❦

We held a small memorial service for Dean in the church, nothing official, just a few of the people who knew him. We lit candles, sang 'Amazing Grace.' Two of us held on to Bryan as he collapsed, sobbing.

Spring came, the investigation went on, and for a while it did not directly touch my life. In May, one of the older men who came round the church had a catastrophic fall down a stairway in his rooming house, the same house Isaac still lives in. While he lay in the hospital on life support, his social worker told me that one of this man's worst fears was of dying alone, and that his mother in Quebec desperately wanted him to receive the sacrament as shortly before death as possible.

So I was there in the room when life support was disconnected; but then he kept on breathing, kept on long past the point when organ donation would have been possible. He was transferred from the ICU to a general ward, kept on breathing for days despite almost no supportive care, the fierce blunt survival instincts of the street refusing to abandon his broken body. The social workers left, having done all that they, in their field, could do. I stayed. It was my work now, and I would not let him die alone. Isaac came to visit him, along with staff from the house, and brought him a little kangaroo stuffy that sat by his bed. I was in his room when a van drove into a crowd of pedestrians in North York, the northern part of Toronto, and though I saw the news on my phone, it took me a long time to understand how serious it was, focused as I was on this small warm place and the breathing of the silent man in the bed.

He died not long before midnight the next day. I was there with him. I gave him consecrated wine on a Q-tip a few moments before his breathing finally stopped. His body went to the coroner, a death that must be investigated, joining the bodies – the remains – of all those men killed in the Village. Joining the bodies of the van-attack victims. All of them still under official care, waiting to be released, caught up in the narrative of violence.

Without a body, and no schedule for the coroner's investigation to conclude, we arranged a memorial service for Isaac's friend at the evening drop-in, and then that day there was a power outage through the whole neighbourhood. We held the service in the dark, recalling or inventing words as we went, his friends and support workers visible to me only as tiny candle flames in a great pool of night.

Meanwhile, assuming, in the first days and hours, that the van attack had some politico-religious motivation, colleagues scrambled to create an interfaith prayer vigil. By the time the vigil happened, it was clear that the driver had been targeting women, and that the attack was impelled by the dark web's whirlpool of misogyny, but few of the speakers knew how to address this, and it became an awkward absence, a silence. Bodies of women, bodies of queer people, homeless people, disappearable, a vacancy.

I would wake in those days from dreams about murder, about cleaning up bloodstains from the church floor and walls.

On Victoria Day weekend, I was cycling along the lakeshore toward the Scarborough Bluffs, with my husband and daughter, when my phone rang. My stepmother told me my father had fallen into some kind of delusional state, maybe related to the severe back pain he'd been having for a while. A few years earlier, after a medical crisis, he'd developed ICU delirium, and my sister and I were the only people he would trust. We flew to Prince Edward Island and spent a long night convincing him to take his medication, not to fling himself out of bed, that he was not in a secret facility where homeless people were tortured but safe in a hospital in Charlottetown. Now my stepmother hoped we could persuade him to co-operate with paramedics. My sister was on a tarmac, about to board a plane to present a paper at a conference in Amsterdam. We alternated phone calls, me standing by the bike path as my family waited, and my sister by the airplane stairs, calling me in between calls to our father, to ask if I thought she should delay her trip. Finally, he agreed that he would go with paramedics to the hospital. 'But I think I am going to regret this terribly,' he said.

He was in hospital for several weeks, phoning me at times sounding like himself, at times confused, paranoid, asking me to call people to come and rescue him. The cause of all this was still unclear. After he was released, I flew out from the sweltering heat of Toronto to visit him in Eldon, the tiny village where he lived, and he was clear in his mind, sitting in his chair reading the *New York Review of Books* and eating slices of apple, but too weak to climb stairs, terribly thin.

We sat in the car while my stepmother went into a store to buy him one of the assistive devices he needed now, and while we waited, he asked quietly, 'So, do you think I'll get through this?' My father knew I never lie, and I could not lie to him then, but the only response I could come up with at first was, *We will all get through this by dying, in the end; there is no other way*. What I said was, 'I think you might get stronger than you are now, for a while. But you may not ever be the same.'

Later in the month, the cadaver dogs came back to Leaside. Forensic investigators spent nine days working on the slope into the ravine. 'Human remains are found virtually every day' of the excavation, said the *Toronto Star*. It was a slope I could see from the Don Valley Trail, just before the intersection where the posters were last summer.

Human remains. Remnants. It means that what is left cannot be called a body. The person who had been Majeed Kayhan has been disassembled, distributed, upon that slope.

I went back to Prince Edward Island in August, and my father was walking a bit, though he had to sit surrounded by cushions because he was so thin there was nothing to protect his bones. We had one dinner by the shore at Point Prim where he was happy, ordered bread pudding for dessert, talked later about how calm and relaxed he had been, but when we went back a second time at the end of my visit, he was more anxious, in more pain.

One day in September he called me triumphantly to announce that he had walked all the way down the lane and back. It was the last piece of good news from him we would ever have. On October 7, he called to say that his doctors had found cancer all through his body. At first he said that I shouldn't come right away, that it could be weeks or longer, but my stepsister, also a doctor, called and told me she had seen the scans, and I should get the first flight I could. I phoned again with my arrival time. 'I love you, Dad,' I told him at the end of the call, something we rarely say in my family. 'That's good,' he said, 'though I don't know if I really deserve the highest type of affection.'

I arrived at the hospital in Montague on a Tuesday morning. The small private room was filled with sunlight. My father was still stunned by the diagnosis, but coherent, able to concentrate. He asked me to read some of my sermons to him. I pulled up my Easter sermons on my laptop, my voice breaking only a few times. By the time my sister arrived that night, he was more confused; he would never have the same focus again. For days, my stepmother and my sister and I sat by his bed and read him poetry, his own and that of others. We took down the clock because it made him anxious. He worried about the septic tank back at his house. My stepsisters visited as often as they could, two of his close friends were almost always there, and the hospital staff let his aging black dog, Star, come in the back door and lie on his bed. My sister and I took breaks to walk together along the Confederation Trail.

Every morning I got up before dawn and watched the sun rise over the Montague River from my hotel room while I drank my coffee, looking out as the fishing boats travelled silently from the harbour. The trees emerged, dark shapes on the bank, while the red-streaked sky was reflected in black water.

At some point during that stretch of days in the hospital, my phone rang, and I took the call in the little family room down the corridor. It was Riley, from TNG. They wanted to know if they could book the church for a memorial service. This was not unusual. TNG often holds memorials in our space. But Riley was hesitant. 'This is a different one,' they said, and seemed, for a moment, not to know how to explain. 'It's a body that's just been released after a long time.' They paused. 'You need to keep this kind of quiet. It's Selim Esen.'

The coroner had finally released his body, along with all the others. We would call it a body now, though we all knew it was not exactly a body, not intact, maybe not even complete. But he would be returned to the care of his community, at last. And this made him, somehow, a body again, restored to a kind of wholeness. The family would fly into Toronto from Turkey. This is where his friends wanted the memorial to be.

We settled on a date and a time, about a week away. I called Janet, the parish administrator; I called Andrea, and asked her, in case I was not there, to work out details in my absence. I took this knowledge back to my father's room.

After nearly a week, my father broke down, could not endure this condition of being unable to stand up, unable to think clearly, able only to lie in bed, prey to anxiety, imagining his own death. He phoned my mother and some of his closest friends to say goodbye. The next day, after reviewing his options with the palliative specialist, he instructed the hospital to discontinue his intravenous fluids and all medications other than pain relief. Tubes and wires gone, we turned his bed to face the window.

It didn't take long after that. He was intermittently conscious for a little while, a day perhaps. The last time he was awake, only my sister and I were there. He argued with us about getting out of bed. We played Bach for him on my sister's phone, the *Goldberg Variations*, written to soothe an insomniac count. He asked for a slice of apple, and my sister fed him homemade applesauce. After that, he was always asleep.

I am very accurate, in a way that frightens me, at predicting when someone will die. On the Monday morning, as I drank my coffee and once again watched the sun rise over the indigo river, I thought that it would be the last time I stood there like that. I took a photograph of one of the fishing boats, a bright jewel in the shadows, moving toward the red dawn. My stepmother had slept in my father's room every night since he was admitted, but that night, my sister and I stayed as well, on the couches in the hospital's family room. I heard a storm begin during the night, beating against the window.

Early Tuesday morning, the wind was fierce outside. My sister went back to the hotel to shower. A close friend of my father's told me I should take a break as well, that it could be days or longer, but I knew it wouldn't be. My stepmother and stepsister were sitting on the couch by the wall, and I was sitting by my father's bed. His breathing changed. He had not moved independently for many hours, but now, slowly, gracefully, he lifted his hands and lay them across his chest. Then he exhaled in a way that I recognized. I whispered the prayers for the moment of death, and then I called my stepsister over. She looked at me, and she knew. Checked for a pulse, and nodded.

It was what we would call a good death. It was perhaps the best possible death – as the deaths of Dean and Selim and the others were perhaps the worst. But it was death still.

On Wednesday night, my sister and I flew back, she to Ottawa, me to Toronto. We sat close together in the airport, phoned our mother, and knew that the small, strange, fierce unit of four people that had been our family would never exist again. A family never fully taken apart by divorce or distance or age was now dissembled in death.

On Friday, it was Selim Esen's funeral.

It was, of course, the story of the day, the funeral of one of the victims of this famous killer. 'At a downtown church,' reports would say, keeping it vague, though the identity of the church is unmistakable from the photographs. Selim's family had requested only two reporters, known and trusted, be admitted to the memorial itself, but many others were outside, and most of my job all afternoon was to keep them at a distance, to prevent them from filming arriving mourners or trying to come inside. Cameras ringed the church at the street corners. In some of the television footage I am visible, standing watch at the door, a tiny figure in black clothing, no one in particular.

The church was full. Selim's friends talked about his intelligence, his humour, his art, about his courage as a gay man who was out even back in Turkey, and how hard he was working to pull his life together, how close he was. The painting he never finished, presented to his brother. At the end of the evening, one of the organizers gave me a small brown envelope of flower seeds for planting, with Andrew Kinsman's recipe for banana bread printed on the back. I carried the envelope with me for several years, as if an urgent need for a banana bread recipe might suddenly break out.

The next week, I would lead a funeral for a young woman who died slowly in a nursing home from a rare degenerative neurological disease. Her friends would bring her body into the church with a Morris dance. The week after that, I would lead my father's funeral.

We came round again to the deep chill of January. During one night of extreme cold, a friend's body was found in his apartment, where, at some time in the previous two weeks, he had hanged himself from a beam. He left a letter, which included a request that we hold a memorial for him at the church. I spent one long night helping to sort through his possessions, and as soon as I entered the apartment, I spotted, on the floor, a medicine bag – at least, such a version of a medicine bag as a non-Indigenous person could have. I could see immediately how it must have fallen from his hands when he dropped. I am the custodian of death, the holder of sacred things. So I was the one to pick up this soft leather bag. It contained a rosary, an angel pin, and three stones – one an earthen red, one black, one crystalline. I wore the bag, with its contents, at my waist during the memorial, and afterwards I gave the rosary to his brother, and the angel pin to a close friend, but no one wanted the stones. I have the three stones and the bag to this day. Dissembled. I hope in kindness.

The next morning, the killer in the Village stood up in court and pled guilty to eight counts of murder, and in exchange, at his sentencing hearing later, was permitted to apply for parole in twenty-five years, when he would be ninety-one years old. It was an end, maybe; or it was simply a way to make some things stop. To make quiet the human remains, so that the world would not have to hear, anymore, the voices crying out from the earth.

We are all broken; and only community has a hope of reassembling us. The activist community around my dead friend, the queer community and its survival through every plague and all the acts of violence, the small communities of my family, Isaac's house, and the church. And if some people, even more marginalized than the others, have found their place of reassembling in a circle of tents, if this has helped them become once again a human body whole, I cannot deny them this.

Easter Homily, 2018

There is darkness, and empty space, a stone torn free, voices, there is a sliver of dawn on the horizon, and confusion, there is running and the rushed exchange of incoherent news, space abandoned, people scattered. Then silence falls as morning fully comes. A pause of held breath and weeping. And there are two people in a garden, and all creation begins again, new, utterly changed.

It is the garden of all the world, and she is all of humanity, Mary Magdalene at the grave. All of us in our frailty, who have seen this world's slow crushing of hope. All of us who stand, beyond hope now, beyond expectation, but never beyond the pain of longing. She knows about failure and betrayal, she is every broken heart. She is all the parents and siblings and partners and friends who have held the bodies, or not even had the bodies to hold – the bodies of Colton Boushie and Tina Fontaine and Stephon Clark, of the John and Jane Does who die in our streets, of all those caught on the wheels of power. But she will not go away.

The desire for God, the mystics say, is the presence of God. Our only doom is to give up that desire, to let the world convince us that there is nothing more to want than what there is, a wasteland of power games and empty prizes, of rivalry and death. That the empty space will always be empty, and we can only cling to tawdry consolations to distract us. But she will not, she will stand, she will fill that empty space with her grief and her love.

It is not easy to believe in resurrection, when we see that often violent wasteland, when we see the old bad stories cycle round and round as if they were eternal. Mary Magdalene did not, at that moment, believe, and sometimes we don't either – after all, there is very little convincing evidence of resurrection in the world today. But still she behaved as if something might happen, as if something could change, and even if she wanted the wrong thing, still she went on wanting. So we too must hold that space, we must stand for as long as it takes.

And when Mary hears the voice behind her, though she mistakes at first who it is, she is not quite wrong – he does come to us as a gardener in a graveyard, the one who works in the dirt where the bodies decay. A gardener who comes into the place of death and begins make it live.

Begins first with the restoration of this Mary, this one who stands. He speaks her name, and she turns.

To be called by your name is no small thing. There are ritual public moments, when a name is spoken, changed, or renewed. And there are the moments, in relationship or in solitude, when we know our selves to be known, intimately known, and changed by that knowing. The moments when we are named, truly named, the names we have always and never had. When the risen presence of the Word comes to us, unimaginable, and speaks, and we turn. We turn toward that love, and our own love is answered. We are restored to our selves. For this is where resurrection, in this world, must start. With us. With you. Right here. Right now. If there is to be resurrection in our time, it must be us.

We must turn, however hard the turning, from the grave to the voice, from grief and loss to the possible human voice which questions us, calls us, names us. We must let ourselves be named. It begins with our choice to be our own selves once again, the selves we were given in our creation, in our own baptism, the difficult, awkward selves we may not even like, who do not fit into this world, who want something more, something better and truer and kinder, the selves whose burned edges hurt, the selves eternally beloved by the rising lamb. There may be no harder thing, sometimes, than to become yourself, in the face of all that would prevent you.

We enter into that love and into our own being, we come back to the garden, that mythical garden of creation and innocence, the legend of humanity's childhood. But, like Mary, we come back changed. We come back knowing good and evil, and more of evil than we wish. And still we come back choosing good, in the face of it all; we come back turning to hope, turning to sunrise, that the garden may yet be made green again. And for one moment the whole long story which brought us here makes sense after all, and we can believe it all redeemed, each wound and each tear, embraced in the great morning of God's story.

It is a moment which is necessarily fragile, fleeting, the movement of a breeze. She cannot hold on to the beloved one who has returned to her. She cannot stay in this garden, for the world needs gardening. The world must be brought back into that constantly moving life, that growth and change and flux which every garden shows us, those self-seeding shoots springing up in rubbish, those perennials stretching beyond any walls we build, the twining life of vines and underground networks of roots. And in this work we are all guerrilla gardeners, throwing seed into the gaps between the concrete. We have no stable home in this world; but we all have our gardens, somewhere, even if they are sometimes very dry, and bringing the green life back a long task.

She has her name, Mary. And she has her work. She is given this, that she will be the first to cast into the world this seed, this news. To be the witness, the one who, in this moment, is the whole of the church that will ever come to be. To say the one thing she can never prove but knows with perfect truth – *I have seen the Lord.*

And it is our task, too, built into the cells of our bodies, laid upon us at baptism, renewed each time we take in our hands the presence of God as bread and wine, the things we take into our perishable bodies and by which we are made and changed. We are sent into this world to plant life in the wasteland. Tell the impossible story: That love is stronger than death, and many waters cannot quench it, and floods cannot drown it. That we are not lost among the graves. Tell it in the face of all the evidence. Tell it even if no one believes you, tell it even if you can hardly believe it yourself. Because without this story, the world is lost. Keep saying this, that our hearts and souls can rise out of the rubble, that life will rise up in the abandoned places, that another world is possible, that we can begin to build that world in the wreckage of this our garden.

We are the witnesses now, whether or not we feel adequate to the task, whether or not we even want it. We have been made and loved and named. Go into the world, live out the story that the hungry will be fed, and the prisoners will be released, and all the designs of power will fail, and the garden will come back to the city, and the green things rise again. Be, your own selves, the truth of that story in this time and in this place. Walk back into the place of murder, and tell them that they will not prevail. It is foolish, and sometimes dangerous, and it doesn't make sense.

Power and greed and fear will try to stop you, time and grief will wear you down. But life stands with you, speaks your name in the morning.

Land

The dimensions of humanity that are disadvantaged or ignored in the world where what matters is managing relations that are always potentially threatening and patrolling territories that are always threatened – these are the dimensions that are accommodated in the life of the Church, in the territory that is not defended or patrolled but claims to be potentially everyone's. And for the Church to make this credible and effective requires of the Church a rigorous collective self-displacement, a readiness constantly to question itself as to how far it has yielded to the temptation of territorial anxiety.

– Rowan Williams

It is maybe too obvious to say, but homeless people, having no homes, also have no privacy. One morning, not an especially unusual morning, I saw someone taken away from the encampment in handcuffs because he had been quietly sharpening a kitchen knife he had inherited from his father, who had been a chef, and someone passing by called 911 to report 'a man with a butcher knife.' If each of us was exposed to a 911 call every time we picked up a knife in our own kitchens, our attitude to the world would not long remain trusting.

All the dysfunction most of us enact behind closed doors takes place in public view; and, similarly, none of us would fare very well if we were permanently in public view, if every time we shouted or cried we had the whole street as an audience. Complaints about the encampment really began in the sweltering summer of 2022, after its swift growth that spring, when a dozen or so tents quickly occupied all the free space, as other encampments were cleared, and as people looking for somewhere to go saw others sleeping, undisturbed, on the steps and by the wall. And at that time, most of the expressed anger involved a couple who had a fantastically toxic relationship – not actually too different from thousands of other couples in the city, but when the temperature is topping 40ºC every day, and two people are screaming and throwing things at each other in the middle of the street at three or four in the morning, or at noon, or at dawn and at sunset, no one is going to be very happy about that. And when this was layered with jackhammers all day long, as the City tore up Bellevue Avenue to replace the sewer lines, and there was concrete dust on everything, and tar melting under the pitiless sun, there was nowhere else for that stress to go, and the people in the tents became, for some housed neighbours, the centre around which all unhappiness turned.

It was during this time that a neighbour on the phone first quoted to me a high-level City staffer (who is now, to be fair, a former high-level City staffer), who had evidently told them that 'these people could be in housing right now, but they don't want to be because they'd rather do drugs,' a statement that is blatantly absurd on multiple levels, not least because the vast majority of drug use happens inside housing, but that would be repeated to me over and over.

My congregation, and I say this with tremendous pride, never hesitated. My congregation, many of them queer, neurodiverse, racialized, knew the community deeply, and maybe even more, knew what it means to be the other. There was never for a moment any question that the people encamped on our lawn were part of us, people we were called to welcome, called to support. And many of our other neighbours were with us – but some were not. Emails started coming in, phone calls to my personal cell number, and I tried to answer, but my answers came from the land of affliction, and the land of the well seemed unable to hear me.

At the beginning of August, a police officer knocked on the door of the church and informed me that I would shortly be summoned to a meeting with neighbours because 'their whole lives are being trashed.' This was the first and last time such a meeting was mentioned, nor was it ever explained to me why the police came to tell me about it. At the end of August, I was invited by the City's Encampment Office to a meeting about what they then called 'the orphaned green space outside St. Stephen's.' At that meeting, we mostly talked about whether they could make arrangements to pick up the residents' garbage.

But at the end of September, a new meeting request came, this time from Transportation Services, and this was when we entered a new phase, the point from which 'ownership' would come to be everything.

❦

The first time I heard a meeting opened with a land acknowledgement, it was at Occupy Toronto in St. James Park. At the time, it seemed like an important gesture. Now it is almost impossible to attend any meeting without a land acknowledgement, in which the names of Indigenous nations are frequently mispronounced, and, not uncommonly, white settlers express how 'thankful' they are to be 'welcomed' to live and work on this land that we straight-up stole from people we killed.

Many people better qualified than I am have written about the complex pre-contact and early colonial history of this bit of land, including the strong possibility that even the name Tkaronto/Toronto was stolen from a different place and applied by colonizers to the area we call Toronto now; including the different stories told by the Anishinaabe and the Haudenosaunee; including the troubling history of the 'Toronto Purchase'/ Treaty 13. Many have written, too, about the deep complicity of the Anglican Church of Canada, which is absolutely undeniable. The Church was involved in genocidal atrocities, and has much to repent, and is still working out the terms of that repentance, although I will note to its small credit that part of my training for ordination included a visit to the Woodland Cultural Centre, which is maintained on the site of one of the most notorious residential schools run by the Anglican Church and includes a museum graphically documenting the abuses and murders that took place. (The grounds of the school are still being searched for bodies; about ninety-seven have been found so far, and it seems certain there will be more.)

It is well-known that a large proportion of homeless people are of Indigenous or partly Indigenous background. Many carry generational trauma from the residential schools and the Sixties Scoop, and some of them have bravely shared that trauma with me in graphic detail. In this context, setting up a tent on public land, and beside a church, is a layered and historically loaded gesture. Yet somehow, every meeting we had with the City opened with a land acknowledgement, but not with any acknowledgement of the fact that we were all arguing about the ownership of a piece of land that had never rightfully belonged to the ancestors of a single one of us on the Zoom call, and that even those whose parents and grandparents arrived here long after colonization was a settled fact were, to some degree, benefiting from the theft of that land.

So when I talk about who owns the churchyard, we need to bear in mind that before any of these discussions, it was stolen, that when the church was built, the building and all the land around it 'belonged' to a slave-owning British military family, and everything else, the entire legal framework of possession, flows out from that.

As I said earlier, in 1858, the boulevard leading through the open fields of the estate toward the Denison mansion ran right outside the church door. As it became no longer an estate but a neighbourhood, easements were granted – or, more likely, just happened – so that Bellevue became a narrow residential street, and the church, and all the houses built on that street, had front yards. But all those front yards remained, in a strictly legal sense, 'City assets,' to use the language now brought before us. This is not particularly unusual in Toronto, or in many other cities. Many people do not, strictly speaking, own their own front yards, and probably aren't even aware of that. On Bellevue, the Montessori school and the Neighbourhood Group daycare created playgrounds, the women's shelter built an artificial hill and picnic tables, people fenced and landscaped their yards. But all of it, officially, 'belongs' to the Department of Transportation. In the fall of 2022, the Department of Transportation, having dragged this information out of the City archives, asserted their claim to the churchyard, and the churchyard alone.

Meanwhile, at the south side of the church, in a narrow, fenced strip that was admitted by Transportation to be 'church property,' V was establishing an increasingly elaborate home. A 2-Spirit Mohawk with intense political awareness and a hot temper, V had come to have a grudging respect for me because I was not afraid of their anger nor likely to become angry in return, was not upset about being filmed on their cellphone, and freely admitted that the Anglican Church was indeed guilty of genocide. We did not agree on all things – I was extremely dubious about their claims that the raspberry bush would 'come back better than ever' after being crushed under a large pile of kitchen equipment for six months, and I proved to be correct about that – but we agreed that the Two Row Wampum was a covenant still in force between white settlers and the Haude-nosaunee Confederacy, binding each nation to travel down the river of life side by side, neither attempting to steer the other's vessel; and sometimes treaty agreements are incarnated in a pile of kitchen equipment on the raspberries.

The whole encampment was, at that time, a site that seemed filled with life. There were paintings and installations leaning against the fence of the neighbouring apartment building, people sitting on the church steps chatting, or listening to music on their phones. Jeff salvaged discarded flags and banners and scarves for decoration. Some encampment residents set up tables along the sidewalk, trying to sell jewellery they'd made from bits and pieces, or else just offering up the still possibly useful items retrieved from the garbage of those who could afford to throw them out. I had discovered, by now, that the Artist was especially fond of chocolate croissants from one of the big coffee chains, so whenever they turned up in our food rescue schedule, I would leave one for her on the arm of the leather chair that also served as her bed. I remember it as being, in some ways, the gentlest and most creative time our encampment has known, although the eruptions of drama from the toxic couple – who persistently refused advice from me, from Streets to Homes, and from TNG, that they would surely be happier apart, or at least taking a break – were unpleasant for everyone. But the machinery of bureaucracy, and the claims of ownership, would move in now, and become the primary theme for the next two years.

When I sent an earlier draft of this book to a friend, she wrote back, 'The overall feeling is of vast impersonal forces sweeping across the encampment, mysterious and unpredictable. Which is probably what it feels like to the residents.' But, in fact, for a great deal of the time, it has also been how things have felt for me. I have no inside information on the City's decisions, and they have been communicated to me erratically, often indirectly, and usually too late. I rarely know who has driven decisions, or why. The structures are not transparent, and, with a few notable exceptions, City staff have not spoken to me as a professional, or as a peer, but mostly as if I were a homeless person who somehow happened to be housed and reachable by phone. I do consider this an honour, though an unintended one, but it means that, for the most part, I cannot tell you who was responsible for decisions, or when, or why. I only know how they were enacted on the ground, and mostly on the physical ground that was the disputed yard.

Everything started to happen very fast; although I have my notes and my emails, it's still sometimes hard to remember the sequences exactly. One day I heard raised voices outside, and found two City staffers, whom we may as well, I guess, call Molly and Polly, and who would become major characters in all our lives, stomping through the encampment, shouting about 'cleaning this whole place out' and trying to grab people's personal belongings. Encampment residents objected, neighbours arrived and started shouting at the City staff, and someone called the police, and by the time Polly and Molly withdrew, the residents were frightened and angry, suddenly on high alert.

At my home, my husband accidentally left our back door open one night, and my tiny, elderly tortoiseshell cat escaped. For three weeks I slept by the back door. The first night, I heard one tiny cry, and ran everywhere trying to locate the source, but then there was nothing. I walked through the alleyways at night and at dawn; I set up a ladder and climbed, under cover of darkness, into my neighbour's backyard to search the abandoned car that was deep among weeds and old planks. I set up trail cameras in the back streets, and spent the days in a haze of exhaustion and grief, sure she was dead, sure that a little senior indoor cat with health conditions could not survive, but still unable to give up. There was snow, there was deep cold, there was nothing, the tracks nearby were skunks and squirrels, there was nothing.

One Friday night, as we tried to close the drop-in during an extreme cold alert, I found a man half-asleep in the chapel, new to me, disoriented, exhausted, not remotely properly dressed for the weather, barely able to get his shoes back on, barely able to walk. There were no warming centres at all that winter, and Central Intake had nothing. All I could do was walk him out to the encampment, wake Jeff up, and ask him if he could take the man into his tent for the night. And Jeff, as he always did when I brought someone to him, promised to look after the man, to find him a blanket, a warm spot to sleep for the night. It was the most, the best, that any of us could do.

And I was coming to work every day aching from fatigue, terrified by my husband's mysterious decline, unsure what to do, how to manage my life, and for all the chaos, and all the days when I had to march up to large men and demand that they hand their weapons over to me, the place I felt closest to safe was with the encampment folks. The place that was honest, transparent, without judgment or expectation, where no one had to pretend to be okay. The place that would always take in a stranger.

On November 23, the fire captain in charge of encampments, a genuinely decent man, warned me that there would be 'a large meeting of City departments' in the churchyard early the next morning. I arrived in the bitter cold at sunrise, and what followed did not in any way resemble a meeting, but more a coordinated raid on the personal belongings of residents, in particular by Molly and Polly, who strode through the camp grabbing at items and shouting, 'Why does he need that?' A senior Neighbourhood Group staffer tried to explain that an old door propped against Jeff's tent was a windbreak, that if you hadn't lived outdoors you couldn't understand, and Molly expressed that she had been camping and therefore knew everything she needed to know. That was the day that a caseworker and I stood by Robin's tent in the cold for hours so that they could continue to protect the grass, the caseworker and I both refusing to move until the City staff were gone. And then, just as suddenly as they had come, the City staff all packed up and went away, never explaining quite why they had come, no communication about whether they might come back.

They left behind Notices of Violation taped to the trees – the first, but far from the last. On these, as on all those to follow, the violation specified was 'dwell in street.' The notice was scheduled to come into force – meaning that an eviction would be, in the City's eyes, legally possible – on December 8.

That seemed like it was a full day already, but then I looked, as I had looked every morning, at the Toronto Animal Services website, and they listed an elderly tortoiseshell, found the previous night in the west downtown, and after a series of frantic calls, I established that my cat – who had almost made it home when she was picked up, in obvious distress, by a kind stranger – was in a shelter in North Toronto, nearly dead, about to be euthanized. My parish administrator Janet and I raced there in Janet's car, picked her up, desperately ill but still able to start purring as I lifted her into my lap. Back downtown to my vet, who started phoning across Southern Ontario for a veterinary ICU that could take her, while I sat on the floor of an examination room, holding her against my chest and crying. It was dark, and it was snowing, by the time another friend drove me to Oakville, and we arrived at the animal hospital and the staff ran out and grabbed her carrier, like a TV show with a stretcher coursing down a hallway. They phoned me three times that night, and every time I thought it would be the worst, but she was still alive in the morning.

Advent began two days later. I went to the Lessons and Carols service at Trinity College, clinging to my phone in case the vet needed to talk to me, and the clear voices of the choir sang the lovely Palestrina responsories. *High and low, rich and poor, one with another.* Candles in the deepening evening. *Tell us, art thou he that should come?*

For the next week, I negotiated with the City during the day and hitched rides to Oakville every night to sit with my frail, starved cat, giving her tiny bits of kitten food on my fingers, watching her gradually become able to totter on her bandaged feet across the floor. Bylaw enforcement came to the church and served us with a series of notices about V's area, demanding the removal of 'debris.' I felt fairly confident that we did not have a consensus of opinion about what was and was not debris.

The evening that my cat came home, I carried her to the shelf in the bedroom clothes cupboard where she liked to sleep, and left a plate of food so she didn't need to try to go up or down stairs, and I woke in the night and heard the sound of a small cat crunching on kibble, and it was such a moment of pure happiness that I've made sure ever since that she has an extra food bowl in the bedroom, so I can wake and hear her eating in the night.

That Sunday, everyone stayed after church to clean up the yard, which had become cluttered with discards, in part because we had, at that time, no regular City garbage pickups. Esther, my choir lead, was photographed by the *Toronto Star* as she gathered litter around the tents, along with several residents. That same Sunday, a friend texted me to say she'd been in communication with Timothy Schmalz, the artist who had created our Homeless Jesus statue, and he had a plan for an installation he was proposing to add to the original sculpture. He thought he could have it in place by Thursday, the day the notice came into effect. And Andrew and I went around to the side of the church and painstakingly negotiated with V about item after item, broken pots and pumpkins and pieces of art.

Maybe this is a good time to talk about the relationship that people have with *things*, and how far it is really just an inflection of our whole society's relationship with things.

Accept, as background, that capitalism depends on a constant flow of consumer goods, and therefore a constant discard of barely used consumer goods; there will always be material flowing downwards, usually in tremendous quantities. Accept that poor people, in particular, will rarely be able to own anything that is sturdy, permanent, well-made, or beautiful. Accept that we all, in our peculiar human way, endow things with our own emotions, our hopes, and our longings. And if your life is all displacement and loss, and you have for a little while a place to be, you will hold on to the broken pots, you will imagine planting the pumpkin seeds next year, you will find beauty in safety pins because you must find beauty where you can.

The extent to which people's relationship to things can be called hoarding varies. Some people are clearly over that line, no longer in control, controlled by things, a small enactment of the principles of our economy but not a healthy way to live. The Artist's desire was, and is, to rescue what may be beautiful from the mountains of trash discarded every day in the neighbourhood, but the intensity of her collecting far outstrips her ability to manage, and her piles of salvage have, over and over, driven her out of her own tent, swamped her living area, left her barely a tiny corner of earth to sit down or sleep.

Others may not be out of control, but everyone is hanging on to things that will eventually be discarded, things they may hope to fix, or only hope to cherish. And the rain falls, and the snow falls, and time and entropy pursue their course, and all things decay. And you are sitting in a tent full of garbage, but to admit that is to accept yet another saga of loss.

And it doesn't help, and says something about all of us, that someone can go into the bins of the apartment building beside the church and, effortlessly, any day of the week, pull out large piles of clothing, oversized children's toys, mattresses, hardcover books, pots and pans and hand blenders and spatulas, all the detritus of a throwaway society.

Complaints about garbage in the street are among those for which I have the most sympathy (as I am also genuinely sorry about our inability to continue our community garden). But I have to acknowledge how much easier it is all made for me – that I create a frightening amount of plastic waste every day, but have the ability to put it out for reliable and uncontroversial collection, with an appropriate number of bins, and a simple graphic calendar provided for my convenience, so that it can go away to the trash mountains in China without my having to think about it; that if something breaks beyond my ability to fix it, or to find someone who can, I can usually afford to buy a replacement; that I can keep, in my house, a substantial quantity of things that have no purpose beyond the fact that I care about them, or that they remind me of people I care about. They will not be destroyed by rain or snow, and no one will come into my house and tell me I have no right to own them. These are luxuries that those of us who are housed in Canada take for granted, and most people have never even thought about what would happen to them if these luxuries were taken away.

We made large clear spaces around V's things, but it wasn't enough for the City, and we came back the next day and worked on it again. A senior staffer at The Neighbourhood Group phoned me while I was in a car, on the way to Oakville again, said that V was endangering everyone in the encampment, that something had to happen, that I had to authorize the City to clear them out – something I was, in this case, able to do, since I was, in the eyes of the legal system, a representative of the owner of that small strip of land at the south side of the church. (Not a representative of God, as the courts generally don't recognize the Creator as a landowner, but of the Anglican

Diocese of Toronto.) And then on Wednesday, December 7, at the very last moment, a truly exceptional Streets to Homes worker grabbed a much-coveted room for V at the Alexandra, a women and non-binary people's shelter-hotel right in the neighbourhood, and they accepted it.

The next day, and not for the last time, we found ourselves at the centre of a support rally we had never planned. What was meant to be a press event with Timothy Schmalz, an Indigenous elder, and our bishop turned out to be possibly a hundred people, filling up the sidewalks, and including a Mennonite choir who had come to sing adapted hymn lyrics about social justice for us. It was gratifying to an extent, that this could happen without us even making an effort, but it was also an exercise in traffic control we hadn't anticipated, and we had to prevent supporters and the press from wandering into the area where people were living, and there is no doubt that it made some neighbours angry, that they perceived it as a protest directed against them.

And the day also included, because politics is what it is, the arrival of a lumpish man on an electric scooter, his face covered with a bandana and a videocam in his hand, shouting that this was actually an 'antifa training camp' disguised as homeless people, and that he alone understood this truth.

It all happened at once: Tim unveiled the steel cage he had placed over Homeless Jesus to represent the criminalization of homelessness, and the bishop spoke, and the press were looking for people to interview, and at the same time City crews were around the back starting to seize everything V had left behind while Andrew and I tried to move everything that might be important into the church or down to the basement, and while the crews were there they decided to seize another, possibly abandoned tent in the backyard, and also cut down all my currant bushes and saskatoon berry trees, for no clear reason other than perhaps as some kind of punishment. And, also at the same time, someone from the Encampment Office was phoning me, offering a weirdly confusing compromise, which was that they would let the encampment alone as long as everyone moved to the south half of the lawn, not for any particular reason, but just because the City said so.

And also again, at the same time, a TNG staffer was trying to explain Robin to the police, and one of the officers from the special mental health response team said, 'Have you tried, like, a fresh start? Like just dropping them in Hamilton and seeing what happens?'

And finally, while all this was going on, a woman stopped me in the parking lot and demanded to talk to me, a neighbour who was finding the screaming couple unbearable; she was afraid of violence, confused, but most of all angry because she didn't want to be someone who turned against vulnerable people, she didn't want to be one of the people who says that other people don't belong, and here she was finding herself in that place. Because it *is* terrible, and it shouldn't be like this, and coming up hard against the truth that we live in a society that will dump people like garbage on the side of the road, and there is no good thing we can do, is an awful moment for anyone who has not been through it yet. And I said something more or less like that, and she started to cry, and I said I never wanted to live in a dystopia either, and yet here we seemed to be, and we talked about why there was nowhere for people to go, and all the things that should exist but don't, and finally she said, 'I need to understand. I need to understand this better. Can I volunteer at your meals?'

So that was that day, December 8, that was one day. We spent the next week making plans with the residents to get everyone onto the south half of the lawn, explaining that there was no actual reason we had to do this, but we had to do this nevertheless. We persuaded Robin to move up into one of the alcoves against the church wall, a tiny spot that was inarguably, in the eyes of the law, our property, and could not be touched without our permission. Jeff, the closest thing we've had to a consistent mayor of the encampment, and his friend Ky developed elaborate plans for reconstructions, and then they were tired or distracted or something, and finally the night before the deadline, they dragged their tent roughly across. The Artist moved a few things to the north side, then moved some of them back, insisted that if anything was inside a tent it should be left alone, because for a while that had been the rule, and it made no sense to her that the rules had suddenly changed. We arrived on the morning of the fifteenth, a morning that started clear and bitterly cold, and found a brand-new tent on the north side, with someone sleeping inside it, and when all other attempts failed, a group of us simply picked up the tent with the newcomer still in it, and carried it to the south, and had just put it down again on the ground on the south side when the City vehicles – Transportation, the Encampment Office, Solid Waste, the police – started coming around the corner.

Freezing rain began, and continued all the rest of the day, and that was the day we first met the Claw.

The Claw, which I believe is technically called a compact excavator, is one of the best-known and most-feared machines in the world of encampments: the City's ground-clearing equipment, the machine that rips tents from their places and drags chairs and backpacks and everything else into trash compactors.

Because it is heavy equipment, and dangerous, City staff insisted that we all had to leave the grounds before the Claw moved in; but residents didn't trust the promises that the south side would be untouched, refused to leave their tents, and some activists whom we had not invited came and blocked the way, loudly, taking dramatic falls in front of their own cameras when the police touched them. Esther, the choir lead, meanwhile, remained quietly on the low concrete curb, not quite among the tents exactly, keeping a sort of letter of the law, staring right through the police officers who came to tell her to move.

Some of us were allowed to stand just outside the main doors of the church, near Robin's tent – Robin themself had walked away earlier, unwilling to be part of the commotion, trusting my promise that I would guard their tent as my highest priority. The Artist was the last to leave the north side, most of her possessions still there. And finally the Claw moved in. It tore though the City-installed metal bollards that had for years divided the yard from the sidewalk and that were never replaced after that day. It entered the encampment, dragging and tearing, emptying the ground, pulling down the banners Jeff had strung from the tree branches, hauling off the old leather armchair in which the Artist slept, leaving only stripped earth and small bits of litter behind.

About a week later, as I was coming into the church, down the walkway between the now very crowded south side, where everyone was living, and the bare ground of the north, the Artist stopped me. 'I just need to tell you something,' she said. 'Sometime soon, you're going to find someone hanging, and his neck is going to be broken. But he won't actually be dead. So the thing is, you just need to help him down, and then he'll be all right.'

'Thank you,' I said, because there was nothing else to say.

Homily for Christmas Midnight Mass, 2022

'And the Word became flesh, and dwelt among us.'

Tomorrow morning we will hear the familiar story, Luke's narrative of the young couple displaced in the city, the barn and the shepherds. But now, at the world's midnight, it is this, the first chapter of John's Gospel, that extraordinary poem, sweeping up Greek philosophy and the Jewish wisdom tradition and the words of Genesis, and staking this incredible claim – that Sophia, Holy Wisdom, the Logos, the Word, the creating voice which moved over the waters of chaos at the moment of creation, has chosen to come as a human body, *our flesh*, and not as a costume, but in the full reality of human weakness, a body which is born in blood and nursed by a human mother, which will know exhaustion and illness and joy and anger, a body with brown skin and black hair, one of an occupied people.

In the old collect for the fourth Sunday of Advent, we pray, 'Raise up thy power, O Lord, and come among us.' And this is that great reversal – that this raising up of power is found in becoming as weak as a human person can be, an infant conceived out of wedlock and born to a young couple lost in the midst of empire, helpless and wordless as any other newborn, crying out for care. Love comes to our condition, John tells us. Love will not let us go. If we are unable to turn to God, then God will turn to us, will come as the child of humanity, so that humanity may become the children of divine love, adopted by the heart of creation, chosen as this child was chosen, despite all good sense and all the suffering, despite it all. For this flesh, this meat and muscle, is now as well the flesh of God, and in our bodies, in all their limitations and pains and joys, we may be brought into that life.

Beloved, you are worth loving, you, all your particular, difficult, struggling self, and this world, for all its terrors, is still the world which God declared to be good, and will not abandon. We too may not know the light when it comes, may not even suspect that coming, but it comes to us and for us regardless. In the sometimes more accurate language of the King James translation, the light shineth in the darkness, and the darkness comprehendeth it not. Cannot understand it, cannot contain it, cannot defeat it. The original Greek contains all the several meanings of this – power cannot overcome this love, because it cannot even understand it, the subversive love which becomes so small.

In this midnight, then, be that light. Be that love, inasmuch as lies within your human ability. Be angry and be kind, be urgent and be patient. Let your body be chosen as love's instrument in the great song. Love is health workers still going to work in the face of a collapsing system, exhaustion, demoralization. Love is continuing to care for other people in a world of self-interest; love is resisting racism, ableism, homophobia, transphobia; love is the baptismal call to strive to respect the dignity of every human person. Love is picking up garbage, wearing a mask, being vaccinated. Love is mutual aid, love is protest, love is coffee and bread and boiled eggs. Love can be very tiring, very boring even, very lonely. But the Word came in loneliness, the city around the stable paying no mind to the infant's cry.

The Word has come to dwell with us. The Greek word is literally something more like 'pitched a tent with us.' When I preached on this reading on Christmas Eve two years ago, I said that 'we are called to love's encampment.' I really did not suppose that we would be called quite so literally as we have been this year. But there is so much hope in the way that this congregation has risen to this challenge, without hesitation, even in the face of hostility, and there is so much hope in the way that the residents of the encampment have supported each other; that, although human lives are always difficult, and living in a tiny dense circle of tents is not how human beings should live, people have struggled through all their circumstances to be kind. This is where the Word has pitched a tiny, human tent.

This is the light coming into the world. Creation is beginning again, unseen by power. The Word which holds us all asks to be held in our arms.

Fire

On New Year's Day, 2023, my honorary assistant Max set the incense burner on fire at Sunday Mass. I inched carefully along the altar, censing it with what amounted to a ball of flames on a metal chain, while Max crept beside me, holding my cloak out of the way. The people in the congregation who didn't know what was happening were amazed at the lovely light effects. This, I guess, was our omen for the year.

A week later, while I was eating dinner, I got an emergency call from a social worker at Sick Kids hospital. All I knew was that a child was dying, that a parent had asked for a baptism, but when I arrived at the floor, I found police officers filling the corridor. In the bed, a tiny figure, unnaturally still, connected to life support. He was two years old. His skull was misshapen and swollen, covered with green and purple bruising. There were the marks of human teeth on his feet. His mother's boyfriend, it was suspected, had beaten him into brain death. The mother was there, thirty-three weeks pregnant, police in the room with her.

I was there to perform a function. I spoke with the mother, I spoke with her friend who was sitting in the room promising to kill the boyfriend if he turned up, I stayed for an hour or so, but really I was only there for one thing. A nurse brought me a bowl filled with water, and I poured water three times over the little disfigured head, and spoke the necessary words. I anointed him with baptismal oil, which is the same movement as anointing the dying. Then I got on my bike and went back to the world.

January and February were bitterly cold. An encampment in deep winter is a subdued place, no one socializing outside the tents, everyone dug in under layers of tarps and cardboard, just trying to make it through. I would run around the yard in snowstorms, distributing handwarmers, blankets, fleece-lined leggings, whatever we could collect. During extreme cold alerts, Ky, an Indigenous man who was housed, but close friends with some people in the encampment, would come in the middle of the night with beef stew and make sure everyone was safe. Molly and Polly visited every week or so, shouting at me that 'these people have to learn the difference between *need* and *want*,' and that I was 'supporting them too much.' Sometimes there were cleanup days, and I would put on my puncture-resistant gloves and climb into abandoned tents to clear out ice-encrusted cardboard insulation and broken furniture and used needles, while Molly and Polly stood across the street, chatting and laughing with the police, and the Artist shouted at people that she was really me, so she was in charge and they had to do what she said, which reflected a touching belief that anyone has ever actually done anything I said.

The Artist got a space in the Alexandra during an extreme cold alert, and went inside, but in probably less than a week she was back on the site. Much later, she would explain to me that she had missed bed checks because she was visiting a friend in the east end and had lost her room because of that.

One Sunday morning I fell down the stairs at home in the dark, and a few days later I was doored by a car while cycling and hit the icy street. I went on from the dooring to a rally at

City Hall about housing policy, but felt so ill that I had to leave early and spend the afternoon sleeping on the couch in the vestry of the church. Rallies and marches had been coming to seem more and more foreign, I stayed more and more in this one place, and did whatever came to my hand there. The Streets to Homes worker at the encampment told me he no longer had any shelter-hotel rooms to offer, because there had been some high-profile assaults on the subway, so all the rooms were reserved for people found on TTC property. He suggested that if people got really cold, they should lie down in a subway station, and then they might get some indoor space.

At the end of January, an encampment in Kitchener won an important precedent, when Justice Valente ruled that it was unconstitutional to evict encampments when there were no shelter beds available. The next year and a half would turn around what 'no shelter beds available' might mean, and as City lawyers and others tried to work out interpretations, communication with us became more and more chaotic. One day our city councillor, now Dianne Saxe, informed me that all the remaining tents would be cleared 'in the next few weeks'; the next day, the Encampment Office informed The Neighbourhood Group that this was by no means anyone's intention, and that the city councillor had 'misunderstood.'

That cold January, one man died in an encampment fire in Liberty Village. This is one of the realities: there have been hundreds of encampment fires, and some deaths. At the same time, there have also, and inevitably, been many hundreds of fires in houses, and the death rate in unlicensed rooming houses without fire alarms is much higher than in encampments.

But all deaths, of course, are terrible. According to one of the many consultants hired to try to guide the City's encampment response, the City's greatest fear around encampments is fire, while the greatest fear of encampment residents is freezing to death. In the extremity of winter, all that people care about is somehow staying warm. All other risks recede.

On the morning of February 4, while volunteers were serving breakfast in the church, Jeff's mattress caught fire. He dragged it outside his tent quickly, and it was extinguished by the fire station across the street; no one was hurt, and even damage to property was minimal. I spent all that day in the underheated church with my coat on, waiting to see if there would be a City response, but it didn't come until Monday, when we were informed that the whole site had been designated a fire hazard, that the Claw was coming back the next morning and would remove anything that was not an inhabited tent, that if anyone was on the yard the police would be called, and that residents would only be permitted to watch from the sidewalk outside the fire station. Jeff took down his tent, threw it onto the north yard as a sacrifice to the Claw. We got through the day.

One afternoon in February, the street nurses from Inner City Health Associates (known as ICHA), a team out of St. Mike's hospital that provides primary care for unhoused people, spent hours on the phone trying to find a bed for a man with an open wound where he had recently lost a finger in an accident. Nothing was available, even for a medical professional looking for a space for an injured patient. City Council voted against opening 24/7 warming centres. People were cold, ill, there was nowhere to go. And all through the early spring, as the cold continued, an older man was burning propane in his tent, and I was confiscating his propane tanks, and he was finding more, and every night as I was leaving, Ky would beg my permission to light a sacred fire on the north side. I couldn't say that it wasn't, in some sense, his land. And I couldn't claim that we hadn't had sacred fires at the church before. Every Easter night, we light the new fire as part of the year's most important service, and at least one year, we kept the fire burning all night, people chopping firewood and feeding in logs and pizza boxes until dawn. When my friend died by suicide in 2018, his memorial at the church had included a twenty-four-hour fire, tended by an elder and a firekeeper. All I could say to Ky was: Not now. Not now. Maybe someday, maybe when things are different. Not now, not when I am watching flame inside someone's tent, and the man in the tent waves a lit blow-torch in my face when I challenge him. Not when the fire captain is here almost every day, fearing a catastrophe.

Fire is holy. Fire is the enemy. Both these things are true.

In an entirely unexpected narrative turn, a John Tory sex scandal broke in the press, and all of a sudden we had an interim mayor and a pending election. It is more than likely that this power vacuum affected how things played out over the coming months.

We reached April, and Easter week. As I was setting up on Maundy Thursday, another call came in from Sick Kids. A girl of thirteen this time, child of two loving parents, who suddenly had a seizure of unknown cause that wouldn't stop, and the heli-copter couldn't reach her town in the snowstorm, so she kept seizing through the hours of an ambulance ride to Toronto, and had only stopped seizing once Sick Kids put her into an induced coma. She'd meant to get baptized soon, her mother told me, she just hadn't gotten around to it yet. So again, I poured water, I said the words, I anointed her, and my part was done.

On Easter night, we lit the new fire on the unoccupied north side of the lawn, but doused it with a bucket of water as soon as the Easter candle had been lighted. Elizabeth, in their role as deacon, carried the candle into the dark church, and I sang the *Exsultet*, the long chant of resurrection. *May the morning star, which never sets, find this flame still burning.* Later, in a haze of exhaustion, I managed to call on my congregation to 'reject the dignity of every human person,' a moment I may never live down.

The next morning, Easter morning, was sunny, almost warm. After the service, we set up tables in the walkway and served coffee and cookies, and the Artist came to me with a huge bouquet of plastic lilies, bound with one of the blue plastic tourniquets usually associated with injectable drugs. 'For the church,' she said. The bouquet is on our small altar still.

Just two days after that, the thing we had been fearing happened. By some mercy, the Artist was out for a walk, very early in the morning, when a propane tank exploded next to her tent, and all her possessions blazed up within seconds. 'I came back, and everything was on fire,' she told me later. The tank was not hers. I suppose that I know whose it was, but nothing will ever be known for sure.

Fire is holy. Fire is the enemy.

Because everyone assumed that someone else had called me, I didn't find out for two hours, and by the time I got there, the lawn was a carbonized mass of sodden damage. One of the trees was scorched black, ten feet up its trunk. There could be no argument about the Claw this time; it arrived by late morning and tore away everything. Streets to Homes workers came, with shelter-hotel rooms suddenly available, and most of the people on the site accepted them. Robin, untouched by the fire, and known even to City workers as one of the most careful people in the community, stayed in their alcove by the wall, and two people moved temporarily into the garden area at the back. For a single day, the Bellevue lawn had no tents on it, neither north nor south side.

A day was about as long as it lasted. Before the City made a decision about whether or not they wanted to put up a fence, tents began to return, because people, as always, had no other real choices. The Artist was, once again, evicted from her hotel room in less than a week for missing a bed check, and came back to us. The people in the garden moved back to the lawn. The distinction between the north and south sides was quietly erased. The City's insistence that people could own only the bare necessities of survival, and then only if they were all stored inside a single tent, reduced the artistic expressiveness of last year's spring – except for the Artist, whose creating and collecting can be restrained by no one. But there was still the woman everyone called Mama sitting in her old chair, leading a circle of conversation, there were people cutting each other's hair, there was Jeff always making sure that everyone was okay, there was community still.

Two days after the fire, the mother of the girl with the unexplained seizure called me. I thought it might be about funeral arrangements. But, in one of those turns of events that never happens, it turned out that the girl had woken up not long after I baptized her, that she was starting to walk again, that she was giving her mother attitude from her hospital bed, that there was every reason to think she would be, after all, perfectly fine. I visited her, once, before she went home. I suppose that I'll never see her again. But sometimes, just sometimes, life hangs on.

In May, during a time when things were at least a little bit quiet, my family and I flew to Prince Edward Island and cycled around the eastern part of the island for a couple of weeks. Everywhere we went, we were in the midst of hurricane damage from the previous fall. Great trees devastated, dunes erased along the north shore, but below the fallen trunks, the pale Jurassic shapes of ferns slowly unfolding, the survivors, so much older than anything human. Marsh marigolds along the stream banks, among the stripped branches. Walking along a cliff trail as a storm gathered, beach heather underfoot, conifers behind me. Sleeping on a couch by an open window, listening all night to the Montague River; cycling in the morning past ruined houses, the Confederation Trail still being repaired along the branch lines, lifting bicycles over fallen trees.

When I came back, it was already summer in Toronto; and Quebec and British Columbia, Alberta and Nova Scotia, were burning.

In June, the air was orange all day, weirdly hazy, and smelled of wildfire and burning plastic, and the weather reports for days read simply, 'Smoke.' We were advised once again to wear masks, to stay indoors. The wildfire smoke crossed the ocean and reached Europe, and whole provinces kept on burning down.

Fire is holy. Fire is the enemy.

Someone filmed the lineup at the food bank across the street and put it up on social media, and suddenly this part of our reality was the story of the day, though the blocks-long line had been there nearly every day for months. For a little while you could hardly go to the food bank without someone trying to film you. But people kept coming, because they had no choice.

During the spring, I had started obsessively watching livestreams from a feral cat rescue facility in British Columbia, and it wasn't until the summer that I realized that part of my obsession was that these few feral cats were, almost alone in the country, receiving the kind of precise and personal care that should be given to all beings by virtue of their creation. Smoke and fire were their constant background, too, but on the livestream gentle people tended to fragile creatures, feeding them and dressing their wounds, paying attention to their traumas, learning the complexities of their lives, realizing that they would make decisions about how they wanted to live their lives, respecting these decisions even if they weren't what the staff wanted, even if a cat with advanced kidney disease wanted to go back to the feral colony to die. If the cat rescue livestream was the only place I could find that kind of care, at least I still knew it was happening somewhere.

Around 1349, during the first and most horrific episode of the Black Death in Europe, John Clyn of the Friars Minor, Kilkenny, wrote a chronicle of events that includes blank pages at the end, and this passage: '... so that the writing does not perish with the writer, or the work fail with the workman, I leave parchment for continuing the work, in case anyone should still be alive in the future.' Some days that summer, I was not even as hopeful as John Clyn. Around the world, it was the hottest summer in all recorded history. Our grocery suppliers were more and more likely to have shortages. Hundreds of refugees were sleeping in the street outside 129 Peter Street.

The straightforward simplicity of the encampment was a relief for me in those days, a few moments here and there of tree-shaded respite, when I could talk to people with no political agendas or complex demands, no judgment, all of us just getting through, sharing our exhaustion and our small hopes.

Crisis intersected with crisis, over and over. Late one humid Friday night, I had to crawl along the filthy church bathroom floor to get into a stall where someone had overdosed, then climb across his unresponsive body so I could unlock the door, drag him out, give him naloxone. A few days later someone went down in the churchyard, but before my colleague and I got there, a small person dressed in black, with dark glasses, had taken control, grabbed a naloxone kit and administered the first dose, assigned my colleague to time doses while I did crowd control. By the time the man who went down was conscious and responding, the small dark person had disappeared. No one was sure who they were. A child of humanity, called to the moment. Everything is always ending.

❦

The population of the encampment peaked that spring and summer, I think, with as many as seventeen tents unbelievably squeezed into the little yard, some with multiple inhabitants, and others sleeping under blankets or cardboard in the walk-ways. At the same time, the intermittent complaints from people living nearby turned into something different, and much more intense, an increasingly organized campaign. Letters began arriving in May from people identifying themselves as staff or parents at the Montessori school two buildings down the block, initially mostly upset about needles, or garbage, or people swearing loudly within the hearing of their children. At the beginning of June, there was one incident that seems to have been genuinely scary, a person on Bellevue, near the encamp-ment, having some kind of psychotic break, who did direct loud verbal abuse at parents and children, apparently calling the children 'fucking crybabies,' among other things. The person was not an encampment resident, and the other residents didn't know who he was. (Admittedly, the Artist identified him as her husband, but most of her relationships take place in other dimensions, so their relevance to this dimension is hard to determine.) The police transported him to the hospital quickly, well before I was even informed. But this single incident would be retold in complaint letters so often it would come to seem that it had happened dozens of times over.

I don't want to talk about this at too great length. I don't want to seem to be naming the Montessori staff and parents as adversaries. Their fear was, and is, utterly real, even if not utterly justified. The level of open affliction put before them in the encampment was genuinely foreign to their world, a world in which conflict and illness are private, hidden things, and it was almost impossible for them to process or understand, registering only as a deliberate horror. And if none of them believe the truth that there are no shelters, that there is no housing, that there are no long-stay treatment facilities for anyone other than the wealthy, that is in part because they have been wilfully misinformed by others with more power. But it is also because they have been prepared to believe the misinformation; because the alternative would be to accept that someone they loved could also end up in this place.

I have talked about shelter myths – maybe this is the place to address some of the persistent myths about mental health and addiction treatment, and in particular the idea that it is, in some way, possible to commit people for long-term treatment against their will, and that I have been actively preventing this outcome for the encampment residents.

The first thing to make clear is that it has been legally imposs-ible to commit someone for treatment involuntarily in Ontario, barring certain very narrowly defined circumstances, for decades, as a result of multiple successful Charter challenges. I am aware, of course, that many politicians are calling for this legislation to be changed, and that the province of British Columbia is already attempting to change it. Involuntary treatment has a poor success rate, and it's quite likely that any expansions of involuntary treat-ment, if they occurred, would be struck down again by the courts; but it would also be extremely expensive, in a context where hospitals are already overloaded, understaffed, and on the verge of being unable to function. The John Howard Society recently estimated the cost per month of a single hospital bed in Ontario at $13,500; this would not include the start-up costs of building new facilities.

Of course, it is quite likely that involuntary 'treatment' facil-ities would actually be run like prisons, and have no real thera-peutic intent, with the sole aim of getting people locked up and out of sight – the proposed new facilities in B.C. are to be built on the grounds of existing prisons. Nevertheless, a single bed in one of Ontario's overcrowded jails still costs $3,960 a month, not including start-up costs – nearly double the cost of a shelter bed, and more than five times the cost of a supportive housing unit. Ontario has shown little interest in expanding shelter beds, and less in supportive housing. A huge expansion of detention/ 'treatment' facilities, especially if they become, as they likely would, places of long-term detention, would come with a massive financial price, not even considering the social price.

It is important to know that, right now, people who deeply and consistently want mental health or addiction treatment are almost always unable to obtain it, unless they are able to pay significantly large sums of money, and no politician seems willing to spend the money needed for a serious expansion of *voluntary* treatment. I speak as someone who has sought fruitlessly through the system for even a detox bed, much less a treatment bed. I speak as someone who has walked people, people who wanted help, into psychiatric emergency departments over and over, seen suicidal friends sent back onto the street against their own desires. I have seen people told they could not receive psychiatric treatment unless they were completely clean of drugs for three months, but given no support in achieving that goal. I have seen others in intensely psychotic states held no longer than forty-eight hours, and someone who had beaten his own skull on the pavement until it broke was back on that same pavement the next day.

It may also be appropriate here to mention that, at this point in the summer, one of my volunteers was on crutches because, while he was working at the hospital, he was assaulted by a middle-class ER patient who was infuriated that another patient he identified as a 'drug addict' was getting care to which he believed himself to be more entitled.

It was at Black Lives Matter protests that I learned the chant 'The system isn't broken, it was built this way.' It applies here, as it applies so many other places – the system was built to ensure that people without the ability to pay also don't have the ability to heal, indeed have a very limited ability even to go on living. And if we as a society are not willing to pay for treatment for people who want it, but decide that we are willing to pay for their long-term detention, then we are making it very clear that the only thing we really want to do is to punish the vulnerable for being vulnerable.

❦

A week later, a right-wing mayoral candidate with the strikingly appropriate name of Anthony Furey held a press conference outside the Montessori school, on the theme of the crime and drug cesspool of Kensington Market in general, and the encampment in particular, and the threat that the whole city would go this way if his tough-on-crime agenda was not implemented. He released photographs of needles and garbage that we presume he obtained from Montessori staff and parents, since they were familiar to us from their complaint letters. The photographs showing large quantities of needles and sharps boxes had been taken on cleanup days, when needles had been collected together in large numbers for safe disposal. Furey also released a video, unfamiliar to us until then, showing a Neighbourhood Group client, not an encampment resident, in a state of crisis, and easily identifiable, perhaps counting on the fact that this person would be too vulnerable to bring legal action.

The next week, in a meeting with Councillor Saxe that would turn out to be surprisingly pivotal, a representative of the Encampment Office, attending by speakerphone, first suggested that the churchyard could be converted into a garden. TNG senior staff and I, after acknowledging that we understood that the City claimed the land and that we had no decision-making power, agreed that, as a long-term goal, if people could be gradually moved into housing and the space was no longer required for anyone to live, this could make sense. I had wanted a garden there for some years, in fact, but had found gardening in an area with heavy shade, and soil deeply infiltrated with tree roots, quite challenging. I mentioned that, some time ago, a few TNG workers and I had talked about a memorial for all the homeless and marginalized people we had lost, how the community needed such a place, whether at the church or in one of the parks, and we'd even drawn up a few plans, back in 2020, before events got ahead of us. It did not occur to us that our city councillor would pick up that ball and make a frantic run with it toward some very notional goalposts.

Then one Sunday, a small group of Montessori staff and parents arrived for Mass. Hostile attendance at services is not unknown at my church. The visit most initially frightening and ultimately bizarre was a literal neo-fascist, who appeared in the congregation one Sunday after we had stood on the opposite side of police barricades for weeks at the anti-Muslim rallies near City Hall, back in 2017. That morning, I was genuinely concerned for my safety at the moments when I had to turn my back to the seats, but he did nothing untoward, and left in the collection plate a scrawled note about wanting to get to know me better, which was perhaps a neo-fascist idea of how dating works. This second encampment spring, the first hostile attenders, on one rainy morning, were the lumpish man I mentioned earlier, who had accused us of being an antifa training camp, and his partner. They appeared to be recording me on their phones in order to expose me in social media, but were probably disappointed to discover that I was not, in fact, calling for an armed anarchist uprising, but mostly talking about the Bible.

Compared to either of these appearances, the Montessori staff and parents who came in the summer were reasonably ordinary; they might have been people who actually wanted to come to church, if it weren't that they came in the doors edgy and defensive, as if they expected me to throw them out, or that they aimed tense unreadable glares at me for most of the service. But we did talk, afterwards, and agreed to arrange a meeting, with parents, school staff, me and Andrew, and two senior staff from The Neighbourhood Group. At the meeting, we talked about working together to lobby the City for more garbage pickup, and the creation of more housing. Any agreements we may have thought we had disappeared, more or less, within hours, probably in part because, as we all came out of the school, we became aware of a major disruption in the encampment.

It is, maybe, an object lesson in how the same situation is perceived by different people. What I saw – a sobbing young woman saying that she had been sexually assaulted, being comforted by a friend; the other encampment residents confining the alleged perpetrator to a tent so he couldn't run away; the police taking nearly a full hour to respond, with the residents continuing to detain the accused person for the entire time, while also calling an ambulance to take the assaulted woman away, and expressing to me their frustration that the police weren't there, and their well-founded certainty that the same call from posh Rosedale would have been dealt with a lot faster. To me, this was a community dealing with the violations that happen in a society full of sexual violence, responding with responsibility, trying to do their level best to ensure that justice could be done. What the Montessori staff and parents saw: that the encampment was filled with rape and violence, and that rape and violence could be ended by ending the encampment.

Within a week, I found a TV crew outside the church, demanding my comments on a press conference that had just taken place at the school, without our knowledge, at which our city councillor had referred to the encampment as a place of 'non-stop crime' that had to be cleared out so that a memorial garden for homeless people could be constructed, comments she then repeated to Marcus Gee from the *Globe and Mail*. Social media blew up a bit at this point, and once the memorial for dead homeless people was so tightly linked to the forcible eviction of living homeless people, there was never any more hope of it coming back as a useful plan.

More notices of violation had been taped to the trees in May and in late June, again giving 'dwell in street' as the offence, the City's way of remaining in the legal position of being able to evict if they chose. On June 27, Olivia Chow was elected as the new mayor of Toronto, scheduled to take office on July 12. On June 28, the Donnie Creek wildfire in British Columbia, on the territory of three First Nations, grew larger than all of Prince Edward Island, and experts predicted that it would continue to burn through the winter. That day Toronto, with our smoke-orange smouldering sky, recorded the worst air quality in the world.

On July 4, Molly informed one of the Neighbourhood Group workers that there would be a forcible clearing on, interestingly enough, July 11, the day before the official transfer of mayoral power. Because I am not averse to pulling strings, and not without my own connections, I spoke to the mayor-elect the next day, and within a few hours received a phone call from the Encampment Office telling me that there would be no forcible clearing on July 11, that there had never been any plan at all for a forcible clearing on July 11, that they could not in any way explain why we had been clearly told that there would be. For the next two weeks we received messages from Montessori parents and their family members, sometimes at the rate of a message every two or three hours, many of them stating that Councillor Dianne Saxe had assured them that the encampment would be cleared on July 11 and expressing their confusion and anger that this had not happened.

Discussions with the City took on an escalating quality of surreality, including one Zoom meeting at which Molly memorably informed us that 'the City only issues tents to people if they go into shelter-hotels,' perhaps so they could set up tents within their rooms – none of us was ever quite sure. Around the same time, one of the community police officers warned me that 'influential people' were circulating a petition demanding that all the encampment residents should be detained and sent to work on farms in Northern Ontario. I never found out anything more about who the influential people were, or how Northern Ontario managed to avoid this probably not very useful influx of forced agricultural labour.

On July 26, a senior staffer at the mayor's office phoned me 'just to clarify something.' According to the staffer, Dianne Saxe had just informed the mayor that I would be completely fine with a forcible encampment clearing. 'We thought that was unlikely,' said the staffer.

Sometimes it's not even a dystopia, because a dystopia would never be this absurd.

Loss

I have talked already about the way that life on the street becomes an infinite litany of loss. From the losses of bags and books and clothing to tents and ID and medications and photographs, all your material possessions are fleeting, even the precious ones – nothing is stable. But it is much more than that. The loss of friends: to overdose, to suicide, to preventable illness. The loss of children: to grandparents or foster families when they are younger, or to estrangement when they are older; nearly everyone on the street has lost at least one child, in at least one of these ways. The loss of stability, of your image of yourself, of anything that brings you satisfaction, the loss of employment, the loss of skills and motivation.

And yet there are always more losses unfolding.

I knew Jeff long before he lived in the yard, back when he shared an apartment with a girlfriend and came every week to a late-night art jam at the church, and as long as I had known him he was always with his adored and adoring dog, a German shepherd cross named Taurus. Taurus was a very good dog, obedient to commands, friendly, much calmer in temperament than Jeff himself; after they ended up in the encampment, Jeff taught Taurus to alert to overdoses, and he became a lifesaving dog. But big dogs have short lives, and Taurus was well into old age now, and it was starting to show. Though he and Jeff could curl up in a sleeping bag together at night and keep each other warm, the dog was finding the cold hard to handle during the day; on the frigid morning in February 2023 when Jeff's mattress caught fire, I brought Taurus into the church, and he slept deeply for hours on a blanket in the warmest room in the building, reluctant to get up even to eat or drink water – though he leapt to his feet when Jeff arrived, and shuffled across the room to him instantly.

We have one regular volunteer, Jocelyn, an older professional woman, who is also a passionate dog person, and able to recognize an extra-good dog and a devoted owner when she sees them. She and Jeff and Taurus became friends, and she began bringing over dog food, and letting them come to her yard, when the hot weather arrived, to cool off with her garden hose.

As the summer went on, we all began to notice that Taurus was losing weight, vomiting often, that his appetite was diminishing. In July, one of the workers at TNG arranged for a vet who provided free care to homeless dogs to assess him, and the news was not good – advanced kidney failure, common in large dogs his age, but untreatable. The only possible goal was to keep him comfortable for the next few months. The vet wrote a prescription for gabapentin, renewable for as long as it was needed.

I started paying visits to Taurus once or twice a day, and the TNG staff let Jeff spend extra time with him in a quiet, private room, normally reserved for overdose recovery. Slowly the dog became less able to eat, even when we provided prescription dog food, even when Jeff used his social assistance money to buy high-quality meat. Taurus was very thin, and some days he couldn't even get to his feet, and Jeff would pick him up and nestle him in a bike trailer and drive him around the city 'so he can smell interesting things.' Sometimes people stole the gabapentin and Jeff had to find ways to renew the prescription early. Jocelyn donated money for medications, for any additional vet care that might help.

And because I am the priest, the custodian of death, it became my job to talk to Jeff about what was coming. At first he couldn't even consider it, was determined to find a miracle cure, thought maybe Taurus had been poisoned by Jeff's ex-girlfriend and could recover with the right antidote, or had worms and just needed some dewormer. But slowly it became possible for me to talk about what he might want, just in case Taurus didn't get better, and slowly we developed plans. He couldn't accept euthanasia. His idea, he said at last, was that if he saw that the time was close, he and Taurus would get on the ferry to Toronto Island and find a private spot with grass and trees and water, and it would quietly happen there.

'I picked him up when he was just born,' Jeff told me. 'And we knew each other right away. We knew we belonged together. I said I'd always protect him.'

Cremation was another thing that wasn't acceptable. Taurus would have to be buried, by Jeff himself. 'We already have one dog buried in the church basement,' I said (which is true, and a whole other long story). 'You could bury him there if you wanted.' Jeff started to cry.

And then things got much, much stranger. Everything that follows sounds so strange that it would seem that it couldn't be true. But multiple people, including police officers, witnessed enough of it that I believe that what I am telling you is, very largely, what actually happened.

One night in late July, Jeff, while out for a walk, was side-swiped by a car and taken to hospital with a fractured leg.

Taurus stayed in the encampment, being tended by friends. When Jeff was discharged, he found a woman he didn't know waiting for him, with Taurus, telling him that both of them could come back to her apartment in Liberty Village to rest for a while.

And yes, many people who usually live their lives in a state of suspicion and hypervigilance can be incredibly naive at just the wrong moment. In pain, probably concussed, Jeff accepted her offer. And the next day, the woman threw him out of her apartment, locked the door, and kept Taurus. He phoned the police and went back to the apartment with police officers. She brandished a piece of paper that, she claimed, showed that Jeff had signed ownership of Taurus over to her.

I found Jeff in the encampment, distraught and confused. 'It was that same woman that took Wendy's dog,' said another resident. 'And the dog from that lady that lives in Bellevue Park. She's taking dogs all the time.'

I tried to phone the number Jeff had for the woman. It was clearly a burner, no longer in operation. Jocelyn phoned the police again, spoke to a sympathetic inspector, gave him my number. He promised to send officers to my house to take my account of events. They arrived late at night, I talked to them on the porch in bare feet so my daughter wouldn't be disturbed, and once they established that I was not personally being threatened by Jeff, they lost interest entirely, and one of them kept saying that the dog had to be dead by now anyway, so why were we even bothering? After twenty minutes of negotiation, they reluctantly agreed to go back to the encampment and talk to Jeff again, though the woman's piece of paper was apparently being treated as definitive. I offered to put on shoes and go up with them, but they told me that would not be welcome.

Fifteen minutes later, Jocelyn, who can see the encampment from her balcony, phoned to tell me that the police were harassing Jeff. Staying on the phone with me, she ran across the street, and I heard her end of the conversation and some of what the police were saying, her attempts to convince them that Jeff wasn't lying or delusional, that no one was accusing him of any crime, and that he would sooner have died himself than handed his dog over to a stranger. Jocelyn is white, educated, presents as a respectable and formidable person, and bit by bit she won them over to taking the whole thing somewhat seriously and being kinder to Jeff, if not quite apologizing, and finally they promised to send someone over to the apartment again the next day.

Monday came, and the caseworkers from TNG took over, people who could show identity cards on lanyards, who held positions with names the police understood, not abstractions like 'priest' or 'friend.' But finally, they too were helpless. They persuaded the police to go back to the apartment twice, but they never found anyone there. They located a vet in Liberty Village who identified Taurus from their description, said that a woman had brought him in, but then decided the vet was too expensive, and went away again. Her address matched the address we had, but this was no use at all. The caseworkers contacted all the animal shelters and Humane Society branches, asked them to call if any dog fitting the description came in, living or dead, but we never heard another thing.

'The last thing I saw was his eyes,' Jeff kept saying. 'The last thing I saw was his eyes when she was shutting the door on me, and he was looking at me like he understood. He was saying, "Help me." And he was saying goodbye.' Unable to put weight on his fractured leg, Jeff borrowed a scooter and spent days and nights riding up and down the streets, convinced that he could find the woman, wherever she was. He slept in snatches in a chair beside the tent of the sweet older woman everyone called Mama, and she and I made him eat small pieces of cheese, drink bottled water.

A little while later, one of our trees collapsed, and we were into a new crisis, but at some point as all those events unrolled, Jeff told me later, the woman came back. She said, 'Your dog died, by the way. If you give me fifty dollars, I'll give you half his ashes.'

And if you are a person with some privilege, who has not spent time in this world, you may not believe any of this story. It is fantastic, it is absurd, but it is the fantastic absurdity of life on the street. It is not incredible that someone would have some mixture of white-saviour complex and a dog resale business, and would snatch dogs from homeless people, maybe even thinking she was doing good. Maybe she believed that Taurus was just underfed, that she would fatten him up and sell him to a housed person, and maybe she thought that would be a humanitarian thing as well as profitable, and when she realized she had a dying dog on her hands, profit stepped up as the leading motive, and she wasn't prepared to do anything but let him die. It is not incredible, it is even normal, that if you live on the street, anything you love may be taken away, for no reason, with no notice, and there will be nothing at all you can do, and if you try to explain, probably no one will think it could be true.

Jeff strongly believes that Taurus is still alive. In March 2024, when I interviewed him for this chapter, he told me that he had heard someone saying that Taurus was alive, that he was being kept in the house of someone not far away, that there was still a chance of finding him. Jeff was very clear that it was important for me to say this, and to let the whole world know that he has not given up on finding his friend.

And we will probably never have certainty. There will never be a body, there will never be a chance to say goodbye. We will probably never really, entirely know. All we know is that life is constant loss.

❦

In the much-disputed yard outside the church, there were four old Norway maples. The Norway maple is considered an invasive species in North America, imported from Europe in the eighteenth century; it is banned for sale in New Hampshire and Massachusetts, and discouraged in other areas. It is not strong wood, it breaks easily, it is capable of choking itself with its own root system, and it prevents the growth of other plants around it, but it tolerates pollution and poor soil, so it continues to be planted in some cities. The four maples in the yard were planted by the City of Toronto decades ago, one of the few times the City acted as the owner of the land, but they were then wholly neglected, even when the church made urgent calls to 311 about cracking branches.

When the young couple tented on the yard right after the Trinity Bellwoods eviction, we had to persuade them to shift their tent after the first night, because they had placed themselves beside the southeast tree, under a large, half-broken branch that could have crashed onto them at any moment, and did fall onto the yard not long after. Once the encampment proper moved in, the trees were incorporated into the community. People hung flags and banners from the branches, or used them to string support ropes for tarps. This was never a particularly reassuring sight, given what we knew about the age and poor condition of the trees. The southeast tree was burned black by the fire in April. But it was the northeast tree that finally gave way most dramatically.

My professional world, at this point, had narrowed to the boundaries of the yard. Between the Montessori parents and staff, the city councillor, the multiple City departments often disagreeing with each other, and the press of emotional and social and medical needs at the door all day long, there was little else I could think about. The nurses from the Inner City Health Associates SCOUT team brought people into the church for private consultations and primary care. The Ve'ahavta van came around twice a week with clothing and harm-reduction supplies. And other less useful forms of 'help' appeared: a store dropping three full crates of rotting peaches and tomatoes onto the street, a bakery delivering huge boxes of stale bread over the protests of the residents, the largely inedible bread left lying out to attract rats and pigeons. A woman who would drive up sometimes in an expensive car and literally throw piles of old clothing out the window, leaving the residents to clean it all up.

On the night of August 3, 2023, hot winds blew hard over the lake from the south. I remember sitting in the chair in my small office at home, on the second floor, wind shaking the windows. I remember eating a piece of white chocolate and feeling as if I were all alone, in the cabin of a ship at sea, or in a treehouse in the woods. Somewhere silent and private and remote, a place of peace at the centre of the wind.

That night, a huge bough from the northeast tree broke, and fell onto the Artist's tent. Ironically, her vast collection of cast-offs, which had caused such ongoing anxiety for the fire captain, probably saved her life, the blow cushioned by layers of material and broken furniture. Again, I got a call in the morning, cycled up to inspect the wreckage. City crews were there within a few hours to pick up the smaller branches that had fallen on the sidewalk, but they wouldn't take the massive branch off her tent. There might be needles, they said. If they crossed the low concrete divider into the lawn, needles might somehow get them. It was pointless to say, yet again, that needles are not animate living beings. Later in the day, while we were prepping food for the drop-in, Andrew and an occasional resident sawed the huge branch into chunks that could be lifted, and carried the remains into the basement in case they were required for inspection.

We had never tried to deny that the trees could be a threat to life – in fact, we'd been asking the City to look at them for years. But a woman had recently been killed by a suddenly falling branch while she was walking in Trinity Bellwoods Park, so City trees were suddenly a crisis everywhere, and our fallen branch a red alert.

The City's first communication about their plans, late on Friday, was that an arborist would come to inspect all the trees, and that, for this inspection to take place, the arborist would require a twenty-metre radius to be fully cleared, of both persons and structures, on every side of each tree. Taken literally, this would have required relocating the church itself, the fence of the apartment building next door, the municipal garbage bin, and a significant amount of roadwork equipment involved in the construction of a separated bike lane, as well as closing both sides of Bellevue and all lanes of College Street to car and pedestrian traffic. What it meant, in fact, was that the encampment, and only the encampment, had to be emptied, for as long as the arborist needed to complete his work. A date for the inspection could not be given to us at that time. Possibly we would be given notice. Maybe not.

Over the next week, a series of phone calls from the Encampment Office proposed to us a variety of possible but unconfirmed inspection dates. Every time, I would go into the encampment and talk to people about a logistical plan. Gabrielle, one of our most organized residents at that time, started carrying a little notebook to record the details of all the possible schedules, and walked around all the tents keeping people informed.

Late in the day on Thursday, August 10, I received a phone call from a senior staffer in the Encampment Office, who I will call, for the sake of maintaining a pattern, Mr. Holly. I was alone in the building, could not have anyone else taking notes, but I recorded the content of the call as soon as it was completed. Mr. Holly informed me, first, that the arborist had already completed his inspection, the twenty-metre radius being apparently not actually required for this. Second, the arborist would be arriving the next morning to work on the damaged tree, and probably the other trees as well. For this work to take place, everyone would be required to leave the site. It would be, he told me, the responsibility of the church and The Neighbourhood Group to ensure that everyone was packed up, that all tents and belongings were removed, and that the site was fully clear, within about fourteen hours of the moment in which he was speaking to me.

He then stated that people would be free to return to the site once the arborist had completed his work. I asked him to repeat this two more times, and specifically asked for confirmation that people could return to *live in their tents* once the work was done. There was no ambiguity in his wording.

I reported this phone call immediately to the churchwardens and to Andrew – as well as to Gabrielle, so she could inform the other residents. The wardens scrambled all evening to complete and sign a letter, which we sent by email to multiple City departments, restating what Mr. Holly had told me, asking to be given an operational plan for the work on the trees that seamlessly adjoined our property, and requesting that the City communicate with us in writing from this point onward, in order to avoid confusion. No City department responded to this letter.

And we were there that morning, Andrew and I from the church, and Tucker, one of the churchwardens, until he had to race to his day job at the Centre for Addiction and Mental Health, and senior staff from TNG, filling bag after bag with possessions, labelling them all, carrying them to the room inside the church notionally rented as a TNG office. We had so many people named Chad living in the encampment at that point that we had to develop a Chad disambiguation strategy, ending up with bags marked 'Mad Chad,' 'Rad Chad,' 'Plaid Chad,' and, in a daring break from pattern, 'Fly Chad.' A dozen bags ended up marked 'Mama,' because she had kindly agreed to assert temporary ownership of any possessions that couldn't be immediately associated with an owner present on the site. We took down and folded up tents and tarps, rolled sleeping bags, carted bicycles and bike trailers inside, and taped labels to each of them, all of this under the eyes of Molly and Polly and several other Encampment Office staff. In the parish hall, TNG peer workers served pizza and coffee to the residents, and in the kitchen, our parish admin-istrator Janet prepared sandwiches for the weekend breakfasts with the help of one volunteer.

We would not touch Robin's tent. We could only count on our certain knowledge that they were staying away that day, and hope that the tent, right up against the wall of the church and as far from the tree as it could get, would be overlooked, mistaken perhaps for a discard.

At some point in the morning, Andrew, who believes in good manners, walked over to Polly, whom he had met many times, to say hello. She immediately turned her name tag back-wards, denied that was her name, denied that she worked for the City, and told him that she was a stranger who just happened to be standing around.

As is common when there are major disruptions, the Streets to Homes workers were suddenly provided with a list of shelter-hotel rooms, which were available only to people living on the site. And, of course, in one of those secrets of the street, one of the ways the system operates that no one wants to admit, people sleeping in doorways or camping elsewhere found out about this, and came and parked themselves in the garden, hoping against hope that this time they might get a room. A few of them did, though one couple arrived to find that their room had been a clerical error, and they had to make their way back downtown again.

But the Artist would not co-operate. She would not allow us to bag and tag any of her belongings. She told us that she understood that she would lose everything, but she would sooner do that than let herself be controlled. Late in the morn-ing, the Claw came around the corner. Community police negotiated with the Artist, finally convinced her to walk away, and a few of us ran to her tent to grab whatever seemed most valuable, some of her paintings and collages, a winter coat. Then the Claw ripped everything else from the earth and deposited it all in a trash compactor.

Jeff, rather than leaving his things in the church, had opted to put everything in a large, if punctured, Zodiac, which he tied to the back of his bicycle and drove around the neighbourhood in circles all day. Apparently, he confided in one worker, a punctured Zodiac is an amazing babe magnet.

The arborist arrived around noon. I will say, at this point, that of all the many City departments I have dealt with, the two that have seemed to be entirely free of ideologies and agendas are Urban Forestry and Solid Waste Management. Urban Forestry wants to look after trees. Solid Waste Management wants to pick up garbage. They have been friendly, they have been professional, and they have had no other discernible interests beyond these. While I was running back and forth with bags of belongings, and fielding dozens of texts from colleagues and press who wanted to know what was happening, Andrew introduced himself to the arborist, asked questions about the trees and their overall state of health, inquired about the likelihood of preserving them, and in short order he and the arborist were friends.

'You'll have to take all of these trees down, obviously,' said Molly, or Polly, intervening in the conversation.

'Well, that one has to go. There's no choice,' said the arborist, looking at the northeast tree. 'It's unbalanced now, it could go over any time. But I can save that one. And that one.' He indicated the northwest and southeast trees. 'They'll need some branches taken off, but they're basically fine.' He looked at the southwest tree, the burned one. 'You know, I don't think that scorching goes too deep. I think we can save it. I'll do some pruning, we'll see next spring, but I think there's a decent possibility it'll come back. I'd like to give it a chance at least.'

'This is definitely going to take all week,' said Polly.

'Nah,' said the arborist. 'I can do it today.'

'It's going to take days,' said Molly. 'You'll have to fence the whole yard over the weekend.'

'No way am I doing that,' said the arborist. 'I want to go home tonight with this job done. I'll just call in a second crew, we'll have it wrapped by 5 p.m., no problem.'

This might be the place, before we go on to the next developments, to talk about the community police officers. And some of what I say may be unexpected from me, someone who has been arrested at protests on dozens of occasions and has campaigned consistently for cutting the police budget – including once being photographed with a scrawled sign reading CAKE FOR POLICE CRUMBS FOR POOR. I am fully aware of, and to a large extent in agreement with, the argument that community officers are intended to be a cosmetic friendly face on the institution that has a monopoly on state-sanctioned deadly force in peacetime. I have witnessed, and filed complaints against, pointless brutality by police officers against our community on multiple occasions. And yet, when I try to think of people in the outside world who have developed some nuanced understanding of the realities of encampment life and judge the residents by the standards of their own world and not some other, I have to admit that the community officers are among the very few who have consistently done so.

Despite a sometimes embarrassing desire to be liked, which led to failed initiatives like Coffee with a Cop at one of the Market cafés (amazingly, it turned out that the inhabitants of the famously lawless Kensington Market were not very inter-ested in having coffee with a cop), the community officers did develop real relationships with encampment residents and other unhoused people. They've been known to knock on my door and bring me out to talk to people in distress, and their presence in the encampment has been low-key, even polite, mostly an exchange of news and opinions – unlike the also frequent visits from regular police officers, who are more inclined to come in making a lot of noise for no reason and insisting that every single bicycle on-site must be hot goods, even when residents can demonstrate legal ownership.

Is it just cover, a way to make state violence seem friendly? Perhaps, in the larger sense. But I am, at this point, prepared to take allies wherever we can find them. (I could also talk about how revolutions have never succeeded without winning the police over to their side, but that is a complex distraction from this story.)

Because their hours are limited, the community officers were not always the police presence at encampment events, but, as it happened, two of them were the officers on duty on the afternoon of the tree. Their primary task was to control foot traffic along Bellevue while the tree was being felled. The rest of us went into the church, as directed, and kept the door closed for a few hours, listening to the chainsaws outside.

When we came out again, the long shadows of an August evening were beginning to gather, and the northeast tree was only a stump, painted hazard orange. Some of the residents gathered around the stump, positioned a chair over it, added some decorations. I cycled home briefly to give my cat her medication, and as I came back, I saw Jeff and his Zodiac riding ahead of me, pulling up to the curb. Others were gathering their folded tents and preparing to reassemble them. Inside the church, the volunteers were doing the final preparations for opening our drop-in dinner.

At that point, Molly walked over to the car where the community officers were sitting, and loudly instructed them to prevent anyone from trying to set up any tents on the site.

And suddenly I was hugging desperate people who were sobbing on the curb, suddenly we were scrambling to make emergency plans for people who had, especially this late in the day, nowhere to go. For Mama, unable to go to a shelter without destroying her rehousing process, and afraid of the consequences if she used a false name and got caught. For Jeff and his babe magnet Zodiac. For all the Chads, for all the people who had acted in good faith, believing the assurances we had been given.

Molly and Polly drove away. Robin came up the back alleyway and slid silently into their tent. The community officers got out of their car and surveyed the scene.

'Well,' one of them announced, 'I guess we're going to go for a coffee now.' They walked away along College Street. 'Might be a while,' the officer added as they passed us.

But still people waited, the police car sitting empty at the side of the street, all of us still suspicious, not sure we weren't being set up again. Friends brought out meals from the drop-in; I ran back and forth between the church and the yard. Social media began to simmer. In the orange light and long shadows of the late-August sunset, the community officers strolled back to their car, got inside saying, 'Well, guess we're off shift now!' waved cheerfully to us, and casually drove away.

And then it was a rush, getting tents up, pulling bags from the church and unpacking. The City's legal documents would later state that 'within a few days' tents were back in the yard; in fact, there were at least six people tenting on the site that same night – as they had been promised they could.

On Wednesday, August 16, I missed the regular Webex meeting between the church, TNG, and City departments, because I was busy dealing with the ongoing emotional fallout from the tree episode. On Friday, August 18, I was told by a TNG worker that a senior city staffer had told them that there was 'a permit for the site' that was 'a done deal' and would lead to eviction very soon. The worker also told me that the staffer had told them that 'Parks had been given control of the site so that they could remove belongings by hand.' I tried to phone Mr. Holly, but he did not return my call. I made contact with City Councillor Alejandra Bravo's chief of staff, who had been helpful to us before; she investigated the issue and told me that there was no permit of any kind for the site at that time, and that there was no record of Parks being 'given control of the site,' whatever that might mean.

A new notice arrived August 22, by registered mail, from Municipal Licensing and Standards, noting that the appearance of our brickwork was unsatisfactory and directing us to restore the entire exterior of the building – a designated heritage property with exceptional requirements for any restoration – within one month or face sanctions. After intervention from Alejandra Bravo's office, the order was withdrawn on August 25, with an apology from a district manager at MLS, who told me it was issued 'in error' by 'an inexperienced inspector' after 'a complaint from a community member.' The complaint, apparently, had been lodged on the same day the tree was cut down.

Heritage would be in touch with us, the district manager said, so we could just wait for their call. I asked if he had any idea when that call might come. 'I mean, they only have like about two people working there,' he said. 'So, you know, I wouldn't be holding my breath.'

'When we think of the word *sacrifice*,' I said to my congregation that Sunday,

we tend to think – and, to be honest, parts of scripture and a great deal of church talk encourage us to think – of a kind of barter with God; a system whereby we give up something precious and important to us in order to secure divine favour or avert divine wrath. If we understand the word that way, then the idea of offering ourselves as a sacrifice is a dreadful one. It suggests that we must give up, must renounce, important aspects of our selves, our beings, in order to placate the hungry God. This is a deal the church has, indeed, often forced upon people – queer people, Indigenous people, even just people who ask too many questions, have been told that they must sacrifice culture or desire or intellect to be acceptable.

But that is not how we are meant to read this sentence. We need to go back to the root of the word, to read it as tied to the word *sanctify*, to make holy, to dedicate. We do not, we are not called to, renounce any part of our selves. Instead, we are called to make holy all that we are. We dedicate ourselves to God as we are, our vocations, our cleverness, such skills and tricks as we each have, such loves and fears; we sanctify them, we make ourselves whole in our dedication to the kingdom.

This is not actually any easier than the barter with God; in fact, it may be much harder, certainly more risky.

To take every part of our selves – to know each part of our selves, in the first place – and to place them all at the service of love, this is an all-encompassing demand, though it may be lived out day to day in very small things. To make holy all our little hopeful works, to set our days and our dreams under the great scope of eternity, to choose to believe that the oppressed and imprisoned children, the endangered children, the children of poverty and loss, will survive, will struggle forward, and that we may be among the hands which help; or that we ourselves may be rescued, lifted up from the marshes, to take our part in the work of liberation …

We are bound, we are constrained, by compassion and justice, by the community of those we care for, and those we hate, and those we do not even know. Constrained by the call to love, by the slow discipline of kindness, or the sudden crisis which compels response, making our way through the schemes of the powers, and holding to whatever vocations we may have or find.

As all this was happening, Douglas too was slipping – rarely at the drop-in anymore, because he couldn't walk that much. One Sunday in October, Andrew called me to say that Douglas was lying on the sidewalk on Oxford Street, would only swear and yell at Andrew, but might talk to me. So I walked over, on a weirdly hot fall day. Douglas was, indeed, lying on the small residential street, shirtless, his limbs stick-thin and his abdomen swollen.

'Okay,' I said, 'so can I call an ambulance?'

'NO, you can NOT call an AMBULANCE,' growled Douglas. 'I'm FINE. I have a PLAN.'

'And what would that plan be then?'

'You don't need to know! You're always trying to help me! I don't need anyone's help!'

While we continued in this vein, the person in front of whose house Douglas was lying came outside and said hopefully, 'If you go and lie in the park across the street, I'll give you ten dollars.'

'I DON'T NEED YOUR DAMNED MONEY!' shouted Douglas.

Finally I left, while he scooted himself on his ass toward Spadina, irrational, angry, and somehow utterly undefeated by the world.

The next Sunday, I found a message on my phone when the service ended, asking me to call an unfamiliar extension at St. Michael's Hospital. I returned the call while I was washing the chalice.

'So, I understand that you know Douglas Varney?' the person at the other end asked.

I said of course I did, that he didn't live in the yard anymore, but I still saw him regularly.

'Yes, that's what we thought,' he said. 'You're all over his file. So ... I'm a doctor in palliative care here at St. Mike's. Douglas was brought here from the street, and he's in critical care right now, and he's not conscious. And we need someone who can make ... I mean, he doesn't have a power of attorney, but you're his religious leader, and you obviously know him well, so we're hoping you're someone who can help to make an important decision.'

I put the chalice down. 'Tell me,' I said.

His kidneys had failed, finally, completely, the doctor said. There was a chance of extending his life for a little while, if they chose dialysis. 'But he'd be hooked up to a machine all the time, and he'd have some pain, and he'd have to be institutionalized. He could never go back to the street. I'm looking at his file, and it seems to me … I don't think he's someone who, if he were in a position to make decisions … someone who would want that.'

I took a deep breath. I remembered all the times I had anticipated a call saying that Douglas was dead. I'd even asked him to carry my number in his pocket, so that someone could always call me. But I had not expected this, not supposed that I would have his life, at the last minute, in my hands. The custodian of death, again, always.

'No,' I said. 'No, living in an institution was his worst fear. He wouldn't want that.'

'Thank you,' said the doctor. 'I mean that. You have just saved him a lot of suffering. Thank you.'

I asked if I could see him. The doctor said he wasn't sure how long it would take to move him from critical care to the palliative floor, but thought it would probably be later that day.

Douglas wasn't awake that day when I came in, but the kind supportive care in the palliative ward allowed him a final rally of nearly a week. Andrew and I alternated visits and negotiated permission for him to have a nicotine patch, to drink hot black coffee. He proudly introduced me to all the staff as his priest. He ate pudding and applesauce, and asked for hot food, but when the staff brought it to him, he couldn't eat. Andrew brought him a radio, I carried a notebook and, at his request, took notes while we talked. He explained to us how he had saved Canada from a conspiracy of feminists, how he had founded the psychiatric survivors' movement. But his brief energy could never have lasted long. By Saturday, he couldn't speak, and was only partly aware of who was with him.

On Sunday, a week after that first call, he was asleep, and didn't really wake up, though he had moments of half-conscious frightened awareness. Andrew and I both found that if we told him where he was, and that he was safe, he would relax and sleep again. We suggested to the nurses that this was the key phrase, that he was safe, this was what he needed to know. *Twenty-four hours*, I thought. *Something like that. Less maybe.* In the coded language of palliative care, I asked the nurse to call me if there was 'any significant change.' I texted my assistant Max and asked him to be on call if last rites were needed during the few hours the next morning when I would be at a different hospital with my husband, who had a CT scan at dawn.

We got back from the scan, and I had no messages, so I took time to make pancakes for my daughter's breakfast, and then I got on my bike and headed to St. Mike's. 'He's been sleeping most of the morning,' said the aide outside the door of Douglas's room. 'But if he wakes up, let me know, and I'll heat up his coffee. I remember he likes it extra hot.'

I walked into the room, and I knew almost immediately. There is a quality to the way a living person lies, and a slightly different quality for a quiet death. I put my hand on his forehead, and it was still warm, but his eyes were open and fixed, and his jaw had dropped. I checked a few pulse points and reached into my pocket for my travel container of oil.

Depart, Christian soul, from this world; in the name of God the Father who created you; in the name of God the Son who redeemed you; in the name of God the Holy Spirit who sustained you in this life. May your rest today be in paradise, and your inheritance with the saints in light.

Then I went outside and said to the aide, 'Um … I don't think he's alive anymore.'

The poor young aide jumped up as if he'd had an electric shock, and ran to find a nurse. I went back into the room with Douglas, and in a little while a nurse came in and explained that she had been with him, that she'd noticed his breathing changing when she did her rounds and sat with him till he died. She had just left the room to make the necessary report when I came in. He had not been alone.

I stayed in the room for a couple of hours. I had to reach all his workers, and give the Public Guardian and Trustee whatever information I had about his long-estranged daughters. The nurse authorized me to open the cabinet in the room and go through the bag of belongings, everything he had been brought in with – urine-soaked clothing, a pair of pretty good shoes, a coat in poor condition. In the pockets of the coat, a handful of paper towels, some cigarette butts, about ten dollars in spare change, and a lighter that still worked. This was what finally remained. I left the clothes to be incinerated, and the spare change for the hospital, and I took the shoes and the lighter for Isaac, who had been the closest thing Douglas had to a friend.

After a while, the body started to make the strange groaning sound that dead bodies can make, and I decided that this would be what I could take as a goodbye. I thanked the nurses for their care, and went down the elevator and out onto the street. It was, as it happened, my birthday.

There always comes one day when 'alive at sunrise' ends.

Law

After the day of the trees, there was a sense of anxiety always in the air, an uncertainty about what the City's next step might be, but it was more than two months in coming, and we had almost started to believe that we had dropped off the official radar again. But late in the afternoon of October 19, Mr. Holly phoned me while I was in the church kitchen with Andrew and another volunteer. 'So I guess this will be bad news from your point of view,' he said, and at that point I put the phone on speaker, and Andrew began to take notes.

The substance of his call was to tell us that the encampment was to be cleared, finally and fully, on Friday, October 27. The reason for this, he stated, was that 'a community group called Friends of Bellevue' had obtained a permit to plant 'a pollinator garden' on the site. This permit, according to him, had been valid since October 10, and 'because of this permit, the group is able to work with the police to clear the site.' According to him, the City's hands were tied by this permit, and there was no alternative but to evict immediately.

We asked how this related to the Kitchener decision, and he said that the City would 'try' to offer shelter-hotel rooms, from their emergency hold-back room supply, to all encampment residents, thereby covering themselves legally. It seems that the City's legal department understood the decision as requiring only that there should be exactly enough rooms for the number of people resident in the encampment, as counted by the City, on the exact day that the eviction was to take place, and the fact that the shelter system was officially running beyond capacity and turning away hundreds of people every night was not relevant. (Later, we would discover the further detail that the City would only count people who were resident *in tents* toward the total required to be offered rooms – anyone in a sleeping bag on the steps, or under a tarp in the laneway, for instance, would not be included in a count, as the City's expressed aim was 'tent reduction.')

By the next morning, I had spoken to several people in the mayor's office, who said they had already intervened with Dianne Saxe's office on several occasions on this issue, and 'might not be able to hold her off forever,' but promised to investigate. The permit could not be found through any search of City documents. I called several people who lived on Bellevue Avenue to ask if a group called Friends of Bellevue had ever approached them, but no one had ever heard of them.

One of our volunteers did some digging on Google and managed to locate a Corporations Canada registration for a group called Friends of Bellevue Parkette. The group had a single director, who was also the director of the Montessori school, and the address of the group was the address of the Montessori school. They had no other officers, no listed membership, no website or social media or public face of any kind, and their rudimentary bylaw offered no process for becoming a member. Their purpose was listed as 'Improving access to areas for play and education for children, youth and adults in and around the Bellevue Parkette in Toronto, Ontario.'

It is possibly relevant that there is no Bellevue Parkette, and there has never been a Bellevue Parkette. There is, as we had been made very aware for the last year, a transportation right-of-way, with an easement for the yard of the church. Parks and Rec has never made any claim on the land at any time, nor has it ever been called a parkette; it was usually called the churchyard (though I occasionally, in a fit of whimsy, referred to it as 'the plaza').

The same day, someone leaked to us a few details from a City-issued media statement, sent to the press but not released to the public, which apparently stated that the permit in question was a street occupation permit, a type of permit that does not have to be publicly listed and involves no public process. Normally, a street occupation permit allows temporary use of a right-of-way for purposes of renovating a building – for instance, putting scaffolding on a street. It is not meant for the construction of a permanent garden.

At that point, I sent an email to a lawyer who happened to have asked us for advice about donating money for the refugees outside 129 Peter Street. Within a few days, with some trepidation but feeling that we had little choice, we had retained the law firm that had won the Kitchener precedent, to seek an injunction against the eviction.

At the same time, we started talking to media. I'd been finding, and having conversations with, the reporters who seemed to me to be informed and sympathetic, ever since the Timothy Schmalz event a year earlier, but I had been quite restrained in communicating with them. I talked to the network that wanted a comment after the press conference at the Montessori school at which Dianne Saxe had spoken, and I participated in an interview with Marcus Gee set up by TNG, but my strategy for the last year had been an attempt to fly under the radar for as long as possible. As long as possible seemed to have come.

After church on Sunday, Andrew and I were interviewed by a CBC reporter and made an unfortunately dishevelled television appearance that got a surprising amount of attention. I also agreed for the first time to talk to NewsTalk 1010, who had been trying to get me on for a year after right-wing radio host Jerry Agar had run what amounted to a hit piece on us. For whatever combination of reasons, the media narrative was now on our side, we were the David facing the Goliath, and it was a chance, at least in fragments, to try to explain – and even more, to try to make it clear that these were people, and our friends, and we were afraid for their safety and even for their lives.

Meanwhile, the lawyers were working. For all their experience in encampment cases, they had not dealt with a group quite like ours, and finding residents who could give affidavits was hard. Robin agreed, but then their anxiety became too intense, and it couldn't happen. The Artist would not sign anything that didn't reflect her own truth, which included the fact that she owned eight hundred houses in other dimensions. Jeff was happy to swear an affidavit, but also insisted that the only housing solution he would accept was a house large enough for him to bring the whole encampment community with him, which on the one hand is a strong statement that people *are* a community, that there is care and concern and love, bonds that can't broken, and that the great impersonal world of social service will not succeed until they understand this; but on the other hand, it was not going to be convincing in a court.

But mostly, what went on day to day was a struggle over the precise interpretation of the Kitchener decision. It was a battle over *exactly* how many people lived in the encampment, how the count was done, what living in the encampment meant.

It was a battle over whether strategically holding back shelter-hotel rooms in that exact number (meaning that others in need might be turned away) constituted adequacy in the shelter system. It was a battle over whether a room in a shelter-hotel, with intense service restrictions and possibly a limited future, constituted an acceptable offer of housing, especially for those people who had been expelled from shelter-hotels repeatedly.

The City, which seemed to imagine that the encampment worked rather like a hotel with a formal check-in, gave us the number of people they believed to be living on-site, which was ten. They were prepared to offer rooms only to those specific, named individuals. But they would not give us the names, so we were unable to compare their list to the reality on the ground, and unable to co-operate in getting even those individuals into rooms.

On October 25, six days after the initial call, and two days after Douglas died, Councillor Bravo's office phoned to tell me that the mayor had intervened and there would be no eviction 'for at least a while,' but she knew no more than I did about what 'a while' might mean.

On October 26 – importantly, a Thursday, a day when we have no open programming – a young man knocked at our door. He had gone to 129 Peter Street looking for a bed for the night and had been sent to our building; he had a map in his hand, showing directions from 129 Peter Street to 103 Bellevue. We had, at that point, not had an overnight program for seven years, and when we did, it was never on Thursdays. The young man had been told nothing about the building except to go there for overnight space. It very much seemed that Peter Street was treating the encampment as a shelter destination, the way hospitals had already, for years, been treating us as a discharge address. Andrew walked the man over to the Scott Mission, which operates outside the City's referral system, but there were no beds there either. When we left, he was talking to the the long-term encampment resident we called Pirate about sharing a tent for the night.

On October 27, the day originally scheduled for eviction, two Streets to Homes workers came, not our regular workers, but two quite young people we had never seen before. They met with Jeff and with Pirate, and with some visitors. They tried to talk to Robin and the Artist, but because they were workers who had never come here before, there was very little trust, and they got no response. The workers told me and Andrew that the City, at that point, had no housing or shelter available for any of the encampment residents. The City had no shelter beds, no shelter-hotel beds, nor any semi-permanent/permanent residences available, and the workers were there just 'gathering information.' They said that it was possible that shelter or shelter-hotel beds might become available, but they were very clear that permanent or semi-permanent housing was not on offer, would not be available, and that residents should stop even thinking about getting housing.

At our drop-in that night, another young man turned up looking for a bed, this time referred on the phone when he called Central Intake. Again, there was nothing we could do, nowhere he could go after closing time except the yard.

On November 3, our lawyers phoned me with an update. The City was now saying that the pollinator garden permit was issued 'in error' and was 'invalid or something,' but, permit and pollinator garden and 'community group' having all vanished, they were now insistent on clearing the encampment immediately due to fire risk. I was told, via the lawyers, that Streets to

Homes would visit on the afternoon of Monday, November 6, to offer shelter-hotel spaces, and to clean up the belongings of anyone who accepted a space.

It was actually November 7 when they began arriving, but from that day until November 10, staff from Streets to Homes and the Encampment Office were in the yard for hours every day, in large numbers, in a way we had never seen before and never saw again. Our regular Streets to Homes worker came, but so did many strangers. Molly and Polly came most days. I was able to gather some information about the list of ten by listening to which names they were calling out as they walked around the yard, and it was clear that some of the people on the list hadn't lived in the encampment for months, and quite a few current residents weren't on the list. The City would not look at the list Andrew and I provided.

Four people took shelter-hotel rooms on November 7. Two of them were people who were 'on the list' but didn't live in the encampment (it's my understanding that sympathetic workers somewhere had probably tipped them off, so they were able to be present in order to get rooms that day, a reasonable adaptation to an unreasonable system). Four other residents asked for rooms, but were told that, according to the City, they didn't actually live in the encampment, whatever their own belief about their living situation might be.

When I interrupted a conversation – because I was not included in any conversations – to let them know that the Artist had been evicted from two shelter-hotels and would not likely be willing to try a third time, one Streets to Homes worker agreed with me and suggested that it would be better to work with her over the longer term, on-site, to look for housing. But Streets to Homes does not make policy.

The two residents who moved out left tents behind, of course. As the City staff packed up, I asked Polly if or when anyone would be removing the tents. She said that no one would, that this could only happen if I could fully empty the site so they could use the Claw, because otherwise the tents were 'too heavy' for City staff to move. I said that there was a very high chance that more people would move into the tents if they were left there.

'It's your job to stop that,' Molly and Polly both responded. 'That's part of the deal.'

After a flurry of exchanges between lawyers, the City reluctantly admitted that compelling me to police the encampment round the clock was not actually 'part of the deal,' but continued to insist that, whatever they might have said about cleanup earlier, City staff could not possibly take down tents or pick up belongings without the use of heavy machinery.

During that same night, the girlfriend of one of the people who'd gone to a hotel returned. He'd taken a couples room so that she could join him, but no one could find her. She was suffering from a serious head injury, and we thought maybe she was in the hospital, but she never made it there, and had been semi-conscious on a bench all day. Arriving in the encampment after dark, disoriented and confused, she crawled into their small, half-collapsed tent. Near dawn, the tent caught fire. It was Jeff who smelled smoke, dragged her out of the tent, put out the fire before firefighters arrived. Later, as she wept and shook and tried to sort through her belongings to join her partner at the hotel, an Encampment Office staffer turned up and told her that she didn't have a room anymore, that the couples room had been cancelled because she hadn't turned up the day before. I got on the phone to Streets to Homes, and within half an hour I learned that this wasn't true, that the room was still waiting for her, but the damage had already been done, and she would not leave the site that day. Her Streets to Homes worker came, tried to get her to the hospital at least, but she was afraid to leave, said that her bail conditions required her to live at 103 Bellevue, that if she left she would go to jail.

Take, then, the absurdity of bail conditions requiring residence in an encampment the City is trying to clear; combine that with a terror of the legal system and the jails so intense it would never occur to her that she could ask for variance, and there is one more reason someone stays in the yard.

I was due to be cross-examined, by Zoom, on the morning of November 10. The day before, at five-thirty in the afternoon, the City finally sent us their list of ten names. My lawyers discussed ways to cross-examine me on the contents, describe what it meant for someone like the Artist to be classified as 'refusing service,' clarify that some people on the list didn't live there, and others lived there who weren't on this list. Then, before my cross-examination started, the City's lawyers announced that they would not consent to enter the list of names into evidence, and, after long argument, the justice of the peace agreed. Not only did my cross-examination not touch on this, the City's lawyers did not, as we had thought, even ask any questions about fire safety measures; instead, the hour was wholly devoted to demonstrating that I did not stand in an official relationship involving formal paperwork to encampment residents, and therefore nothing I said about the encampment could be considered reliable or admissible.

After the cross-examination, which I did from my home office, I walked up the street to the church and found the Artist organizing some of her belongings. I gave her as much of an update as I could, on the hearings, on the mysterious list of ten names. She nodded and looked out over the street.

'The bodies are all accounted for,' she said. 'They just don't know it yet.'

That same day, we received an email from someone else at Shelter Services. Earlier in the fall, in response to a City call for expressions of interest, we, like a number of other Anglican and other churches, had applied to act as a warming centre during extreme cold alerts. The email informed us that 'at this time, we have selected our sites for the 2023–2024 winter season,' a typically indirect way of saying that we had been, for whatever reason, deemed unsuitable. So, I later learned, had almost every other church that had applied. We were never officially told why, but the primary breaking point when we were inspected seemed to be the lack of private facilities for on-site City staff.

The woman with the head injury had finally made her way to the shelter-hotel, and a single volunteer, using only his hands and a penknife, removed the tent that had been deemed too heavy and too dangerous for City workers to touch. Two days later, he did the same with the other vacated tent. Another person, new to us, a friendly and polite young man, moved almost immediately into that space.

Once my cross-examination was finished, all the extra Streets to Homes workers vanished, and so did the shelter-hotel rooms. Our regular worker, who kept coming, tried to find a room for the new person, but there was no longer anything to be offered.

The same day, our lawyers presented a settlement offer – given that the City's only expressed concern now was fire safety, we would agree to help the residents move off the site for a day, as we had during the tree work, and allow them full access to the site, and to any material remaining on the site, to conduct whatever risk mitigation they wished. We knew that this meant that the Artist would lose her possessions again, and that we were making this offer without her consent; it wasn't ethically clean. But we agreed to make the offer. The City rejected it.

Ten days passed. Our lawyers cross-examined the City's witnesses, but these hearings were not open, so I can't tell you what happened. I spent some of my time trying to obtain documentation that one of the men in the encampment was, in fact, homeless, since the City's database had failed to register his eviction from housing six months earlier, so he could not go into a shelter. The City threatened to seek costs against us if we lost. Our lawyers fought this, while we continued to fundraise desperately to cover our basic legal costs. And the Diocese of Toronto stepped up, put a donation portal up on their website, told us that if our fundraising fell short, there would be things that could be done. The whole Anglican Church in Toronto had our backs now, an experience we honestly had not expected.

I went up to a hotel in Richmond Hill for diocesan Synod – basically an Anglican AGM – and spent two days taking calls from lawyers in the hallways. The City made a counter-offer, which, stripped of legal language, was an offer to give us forty-eight hours' notice before everyone had to leave the site. I felt I could act on behalf of the residents in turning this offer down.

Late in the morning on Wednesday, November 22, we were informed that the justice of the peace had ruled against us. There would be no injunction.

❦

The same day that the judgment came down, around six that afternoon, while I was walking my daughter to a takeout restaurant, Mr. Holly from the Encampment Office phoned me again. The encampment was to be cleared on Friday morning, less than forty hours away, and a fence would be erected around the entire City-owned area. I asked for assurances that church property – meaning, really, Robin's tent – would not be touched. His answers were ambiguous, a probable assurance, but also a warning that nothing could be counted on. At the same time, City workers were in the encampment, telling residents the same thing.

A person close to the mayor's office phoned me a few minutes later. 'I'm sorry,' they said. 'We've done everything we can. Even the mayor can't overrule the fire marshal. I'm so sorry.'

Thursday, in the encampment. Some people were already moving out; others were digging in. Jeff would not leave. The Artist would not leave. We assured Robin that their tent was under our protection, that we would do whatever we had to in order to safeguard it. Social workers phoned me to try to make urgent plans for their people, sketching out how much room there was on church property, who might have priority for which areas. A source called to tell me that things would not start at 9 a.m., as we had been told, but an hour earlier; but since we had already made plans to have people on-site from dawn, it didn't really matter. By afternoon, press calls started coming in, apparently in response to a City media advisory stating that they would be 'servicing the encampment' the next morning. That same day, I finished the paperwork allowing me to bury Douglas, so I was also working on funeral plans. We made arrangements to prepare meals and run our Friday drop-in dinner with half our core people out in the yard. I tried to keep everyone off social media, not wanting the whole world in attendance, not wanting Lamport Stadium here. In the evening, our Advent education series was cut short by requests for me to do what seemed like a dozen media interviews on Zoom.

I went home for a few hours, but I was back at the church by 5 a.m. It was dark, it was quiet. Most of the people we'd invited – church people mostly, and some from Community Peacemaker Teams, an international non-violent accompaniment organization that has an office in the church – came around seven. The sun was up now, but it was very cold. Nurses from Inner City Health Associates came, in case they were needed. Reporters and photographers eventually. And then, at 9 a.m., the City workers, Streets to Homes and the Encampment Office first, inevitably including Molly and Polly, among others.

The City's line, as I understand it, is that they spent the day 'encouraging' people to go indoors. Given that people had already been told that they would be removed if they didn't go voluntarily, given that fencing the yard had already been explained as the goal, it could only be called encouragement of a particularly forceful type. The magic supply of shelter-hotel rooms had opened up again that morning – meaning that the people who left on Wednesday night and were now camping in other parks were never offered anything; meaning that the workers around the city who had been calling shelters the night before, and been informed that there was nothing available, were in effect misled. We do know that hundreds of calls to Central Intake had been 'unmatched with shelter' that night.

Some people had been wanting shelter-hotel rooms for a long time and seized their chance now to take one. Others accepted because they felt they had no choice, and didn't last there long. Everywhere that morning there was a sense of rush, of pressure, of City workers telling you to pack a bag, get in a taxi, go, move, as quickly as possible. The machines had a deadline.

All day a truck loaded with fencing inched up College, closer and closer to us, retaining some odd pretence of being out of sight, and people were texting me with sightings of multiple large garbage loaders, sightings of police vans, sightings of the Claw, staged all around the perimeter of the Market.

Someone new in the encampment, not well known to us, overdosed in a tent (this is a common occurrence during City actions; people feel they need to use their whole supply on the spot, in case it's confiscated or lost or stolen). Another resident got in and administered naloxone, brought the person back, supported by TNG and the nurses. But then someone else called 911, and emergency vehicles came screeching up, press cameras swung around to them, someone even tried to push their camera into the tent.

Andrew set up a cryptic information booth beside Homeless Jesus, with a sort of Lucy van Pelt desk and a large sign reading HEY SIRI, PLAY 'UNDER PRESSURE.' This proved to be less useful to media and inquiring neighbours than one might have hoped, but added to the overall atmosphere of the day.

By early afternoon, many of our supporters had to leave, and some of the press, though other people were seeing the story on the news and arriving. The Encampment Office staff were becoming more anxious, looking at watches, making phone calls, probably to the people who controlled the machines and their schedules. A man sat down on the north lawn, shivering with cold and pain, open sores on his legs. I called over an ICHA nurse, who began to dress the man's sores, and suddenly a passerby was filming him and screaming that the nurse was assaulting the man, calling 911 and demanding 'medical care' and police. That the ICHA nurse happened to be a brown-skinned man was probably not irrelevant in this. I tried to yell to the 911 dispatcher through the angry man's cellphone, while the nurse kept working, calmly, quietly, as if none of this was going on. Eventually the angry passerby stormed off to be angry about something else, somewhere else, and two police officers trotted over from across the street to register a perfunctory response to the 911 call and go away again.

Then an Encampment Office worker called me urgently to Jeff's tent. We had known, all day, that Jeff's plan was to stay where he was on the south plot, that he had gathered a small group of friends who were planning to surround him there, that he had notions about fencing himself in or tying himself down. But now he was curled up in the tent weeping, crying out in pain, clutching his leg, he was grey and ill-looking, shivering, frozen, nearly incoherent. I waved the nurse over, and he crawled into the tent and examined him, said that there didn't seem to be anything seriously physically wrong.

I crawled into the tent myself. 'Hey,' I said, 'Hey, Jeff. It's Mother Maggie.'

'Mother Maggie … ' Jeff curled himself up further. 'My leg hurts so much. I can't stand it. I miss Taurus,' he sobbed. 'I miss him so much.'

'I know. I know. It's all terrible.'

'I don't feel right. Somebody drugged me. Somebody gave me something. Oh God, I'm so cold.'

He couldn't stay there. We negotiated with the Encampment Office worker, who knew Jeff and was genuinely concerned. 'Is there anywhere on church property we can move him?' he asked.

Robin was tucked into the south alcove, untouchable. The north alcove we had already reserved for the Artist; we had already told her to fall back there if she had to. 'There's the strip along the north side of the church. But it's right on College Street, and it's pretty narrow.'

'I'll go there,' said Jeff.

'Listen, buddy,' said the Encampment Office worker. 'You go into the church and lie down. We'll move your stuff. I promise you we will.'

So I got Jeff's arm over my shoulder and led him out. 'I hope no one's lying to me,' he muttered.

'I don't lie, Jeff,' I said. 'You know I don't lie.'

'Everybody lies, Maggie.'

But he went with me into the church, and he didn't get six steps past the door before he collapsed. Andrew and I covered him with a blanket, left water and food lying beside his head.

For the next hour, City workers and encampment residents carried armload after armload of possessions over to the small patch of earth beside Homeless Jesus and heaped them up there. No one was sure what was Jeff's and what wasn't, so they just took everything, piled it all up, a chaotic mountain of stuff, burying the Jesus statue almost completely, with one small new tent set neatly beside it all.

Only the Artist was left now. She knew the alcove was available. She also knew there were people who would surround her if she asked for that. She wanted neither of those things. She had been moved from the north patch to the south, then back to the north again; she had been sent to shelter-hotels and sent away. 'They keep changing the rules and procedures,' she told a reporter. 'It's just very exhausting and frustrating.' This was her home, the one place that had never asked her to leave. She was making her stand here, and she was going to make it alone.

It was late afternoon now. City workers huddled, consulted. The fencing truck inched closer. The community police arrived. We could see calls coming in to the City staff cellphones, see angry debates, but we had no idea of what was going on.

Polly walked over to the Artist's tent and handed her a notice of trespass, telling her this meant she could be arrested and removed by police. The Artist took the paper, studied it, said, 'You've got my name wrong,' and handed it back.

'It doesn't matter if you hand it back!' shouted Polly. 'We can still have you arrested!'

The community police officers moved off to the side. 'We're not going to be dragging her out of her tent,' one of them told me quietly. 'That is not what we're here for. That is not what we're about.'

The sun started to set. The fencing truck was right across the street now. More calls coming in to cellphones, more angry huddles in the parking lot of the fire station. Still under the eyes of the press, under the eyes of a crowd of supporters that was growing again as people got off work. I did not witness this, but I am told that a senior staffer was overheard to say, at one point in the early evening, 'We're trying figure out what's the greater threat here, fire or the optics.'

It was dark, it was cold, guests were inside the drop-in eating dinner. The *Toronto Star* reporter was still there, a CP photographer was still there, a feature writer from the *Globe* left and came back. A senior City staffer came to us with a new plan. The Claw would come now, although we'd been told previously that it could not be used after dark. But only the south plot would be cleared. The north plot, where the Artist was still sitting, would be left untouched. 'For now,' he added. 'We won't touch it for now.'

We brought hot water bottles and French vanilla coffee and vegetarian curry to the Artist, as she wrapped herself in blankets and quietly whispered prayers. And in the dark, the massive Claw was driven through a narrow residential street, to scrape all signs of human occupation from half of the churchyard.

In the other half of the yard, I stood beside the Artist, protected by a patio umbrella from the possibility of falling debris, watching. Supporters blocked the Claw for a while, and others, guided by Pirate, used the time to gather up the belongings of the people who had been hastily dispersed. The Claw moved back and forth across the small street, and neighbours, seeing it from their windows, ran down from the apartment building next door to join our supporters.

There were moments of near-slapstick, when it became apparent that the Claw, parked in the street where it was, created an obstruction to the fire engines, which had to get out to respond to calls, so the Claw had to pull back; it withdrew, manoeuvred awkwardly along the little street, and collided with the car of at least one resident, who came running out to demand insurance information.

Then a fleet of bicycle cops suddenly pulled up across the street, twenty or more. As supporters stood in the street, they began a slow advance. A community officer pulled me aside. 'I don't know what the plan is,' he whispered. 'This is not our plan. But listen – if *anything* makes you feel unsafe, you come to us. We will get you out.'

My phone rang.

'I'm calling with a message from Councillor Bravo's office,' said the person at the other end. 'No one is going to be arrested tonight. That's an assurance I can give you.'

The bicycle cops did not advance further. They, too, stayed in the middle of the street. Finally, when it seemed that everything of value had been collected, supporters withdrew to the north plot, and the Claw moved in.

While the Claw did its work in darkness, Andrew and I went into the parish hall to check on Jeff. He was sitting at a table now, his head on his folded arms, but he was still only just conscious, sluggish, confused, and it did seem quite likely that he, not normally a heavy drug user, had taken something bad, or at least something unfamiliar. More likely the standard contamination of street drugs than a deliberate attempt to incapacitate him, but perhaps that isn't relevant – the effect was about the same. We offered to walk him to the hospital, or even get a taxi, but he wouldn't go, wanted only to be helped out the door to his tent beside Homeless Jesus.

By the time the drop-in was closing for the night, the earth had been scraped, and one of the Encampment Office senior staff came over to me, where I was standing in the doorway. 'So,' he said, 'what I'm wondering is how we can make the site secure for the night, you know? Because there could be, like, needles and broken glass that need to cleaned up, and we don't want anyone to get hurt overnight, do we? So I'm wondering what the plan might be for that.'

'Well,' I said, 'since you've had a truck full of fencing parked across the street for the last six hours already, I'm kind of assuming that's your plan.'

He narrowed his eyes and walked away.

And, of course, the fence went up immediately, an eight-foot security fence, sunk deep in the ground, bolted together, something that would require special equipment to remove, clearly not a temporary measure before a notional cleanup. We stood and watched it block off the area that had been a safe space for so long, a refuge long before I came. We stood in the doorway until the last City worker left, and the bicycle police rode away, and the Artist was alone, in her tent in the cold night, steadfast.

So that was Friday. On Saturday, I took my cat to the vet for a checkup while fielding media follow-up calls. On Sunday, in one of the ironies of the lectionary, it was the feast called Reign of Christ, and I preached on the gospel given for the day, the parable of the sheep and the goats, the one in which privileged people, called to judgment, ask when it could have been that they saw Jesus and failed to feed him, visit him, give him clothing, and are told, *Whatever you did not do to one of the least of these, you did not do to me.*

'And still,' I said, in a church now facing an eight-foot fence,

we must hold on to the vision of that kingdom, a kingdom not like any kingdom or any kind of state we know now, but a kingdom which is more like a body – a kingdom, in fact, which *is* a body, a body in need of food and clothing and gentleness. The body of Christ, as it comes to us in the bodies of those we encounter. The body of Christ as we can see it – sometimes, in glimpses – in gatherings of human bodies, in those moments when people have come together not to fight against each other or against some enemy, but to share in common work and common being, as the parts of a body share a common life.

The sheep in Matthew's parable, when they fed the hungry and tended to the sick, were not thinking about 'doing good,' they weren't thinking about Jesus, they don't even remember what it is they did exactly when they're told about it. They simply saw what was in front of them and did what seemed best to do in their given moment, and did it not because they thought they should but because, on some level or other, it was what they wanted to do.

Sometime in the next few chaotic days, Dianne Saxe spoke at a Carbon Leadership Forum, and an audience member challenged her about the action at the encampment. According to a witness, she responded that it was 'the fault of those people in the encampment who rape and stab and start fires.' The event wasn't taped, and I cannot be certain those words were said, but when Andrew went to Saxe's office to say that he felt that the statement was libellous not only against the encampment residents but against all of us who worked with them, her chief of staff made no attempt to deny that she had said it.

I thought the City might come for the Artist on Monday, but that was not what happened. I put my head out the door, after a meeting about data collection around the deaths of homeless people, and I did see City crews across the street, but they didn't seem to be gathering for any use of force. I went over to ask them what their plan was.

'We thought you knew the plan,' a supervisor said. 'We're putting those concrete blocks in the yard.' He waved to a truck-load of massive blocks on College Street. And that is what they did, for the next few hours – they opened the fence and swung one giant block after another onto the south plot. Some neighbours came and stood in the way for a while. No one was arrested, but when, during what seemed to be a break in the work, I went into the enclosure to offer cake slices to some community activists who were sitting chatting on the blocks, one police officer lost his patience and demanded that we should all be physically removed. The community officers moved in immediately and escorted me down from the blocks with such delicate care that it was actually embarrassing, while the impatient officer roughly dragged out and questioned a community organizer, whom he had incorrectly decided was some kind of ringleader, and whose name he consistently mispronounced.

'Oh my God,' cried one of my volunteers, as he arrived to deliver a food donation. 'They're compressing the roots of the trees! This is terrible! My wife works in urban forestry, I'm getting her onto this right away.' And I gather that, by the end of the day, the City had received hundreds of complaints about the effect of the concrete blocks on our sad old Norway maples. On Wednesday, the crews came back, opened the fence again and reorganized the blocks so the roots of the east tree had some breathing space, but left the burnt tree on the west side surrounded, writing it off despite the arborist's earlier opinion.

But apparently that opinion was not un-heeded, because on Thursday the crews were back again, looking by now extremely grumpy, to rearrange the blocks once more around the burnt tree.

'That's the plan for today,' said the supervisor. 'Don't ask me the plan for tomorrow. I don't even know anymore.'

In a final grace note, as people milled around the fence, and the workers kept shifting the blocks, someone rode up to the curb – Chaz, the Former Agent of Chaos, the person who had single-handedly shut down our overnight operations, now housed, now trained as a peer worker, on a battered but functional moped, with a little fluffy dog peering perkily from the front basket. He stopped for a moment, shook his head sadly at the folly of humanity, and went off on his way.

And it was morning and it was evening, the sixth day.

Absence

Life refuses a narrative shape, and no one ever knows quite how to handle that. Rather as COVID was meant to go away after we had a vaccine, allowing 'normal life' and the operations of capitalism to resume unchecked, so the encampment was meant to be cleared in November 2023, and in both cases, it seems like everyone with authority or influence just decided to behave as if the story were true. Whether we were an arc of brave, doomed defiance, or just stubborn wrong-headedness, we were meant to *end*. Media, maybe especially the most sympathetic media, immediately started to speak and write about our encampment in the past tense. Meetings with the City stopped. Garbage collection was cut back. The only municipal staff who continued to communicate with us were the fire captain, who has always been a man with his own peculiar integrity and individual protocols, and the police. And there we were, with one half of our lawn looking like a gigantic Minecraft game, albeit increasingly filled with garbage that people threw over the fence, and the rest of it still a home.

It took less than a week for Jeff to move his tent from the College Street strip back onto the north plot, and within a few days after that more people started putting up tents there as well. But things were different, in a way that was hard to define. Partly, it was because both Jeff and the Artist were struggling emotionally. The stress and chaos of the non-eviction, combined in Jeff's case with the loss of Taurus, seems to have sent them both into a downward spiral. Jeff was frequently too depressed even to get out of his tent. Then one week he suddenly wasn't around anymore, and no one seemed to know where he had gone. Our hope was that he had gone to stay with family; Jeff was less vulnerable than many, a survivor, so it seemed like he would have found somewhere to be if he wasn't here. But we couldn't be sure.

With Jeff gone, the de facto mayor became Pirate, a long-term though intermittent resident, charming in the way you might expect from his name, good with his hands and full of plans for building wooden shelters from old flats, but lacking Jeff's universal generosity and powerful vision of community. Some people began to think about moving on, though others arrived.

The Artist became even more disorganized, her huge piles of rescued belongings even more built up and then neglected, scattered across the area, blocking much of the yard. She was assigned a new mental health worker, who quickly formed her for an alleged incident of self-harm she has always denied (a denial I'm inclined to believe, as she usually cheerfully admits to 'self-destructive' actions, but explains why they make sense in her own cosmos). What this meant in practice is that she was taken out of the encampment in handcuffs, and spent about twelve hours handcuffed in the triage area at Toronto Western Hospital before being admitted to psychiatric emergency, where she was uncuffed at least, but had to sleep on the floor because there were no more available beds in the desperately under-staffed unit, and where for a day she sat in a puddle of her own blood because her period had just started, and no one was available to find menstrual products for her. Andrew and I visited her, brought her muffins. A day after that, she was released, without a treatment plan or any significant change in any of her circumstances except that she had lost trust in her mental health worker. She spent more time away, and eventually settled into another encampment, south of Queen Street. Everything felt less like a community, more atomized, more transient, the standing tents occupied by a series of people who came and went.

Several of the TNG staff with whom I'd worked most closely went away on stress leave. You don't go into this line of work without knowing that you are going to be broken to pieces – by trying to work within an inhumane and sometimes incomprehensible system, by coming to care about people and seeing them abused, treated like throwaways, seeing them suffer and bleed and die. But knowing how it will be does not change the fact that it will break you.

Robin alone seemed unchanged, and almost untouched by events, in their retreat against the wall; private, monastic, their feelings deep and secret. At Christmas, they came to the drop-in with a handmade card addressed to 'Mother Maggie and St. Stephen's,' and it was one of the loveliest things I have ever received: a winter-night landscape they had painted on a bit of card stock, all dark blue and green and subdued white, and inside a long message telling us again how grateful they were to live here, and signing themself 'R in the Fields.'

In early December, we buried Douglas. There had been some delay because no one was certain who was doing the next-of-kin search; ultimately, I spoke to the police, and they did a web search based on the sparse information I could give them, and concluded, to no one's surprise, that his daughters

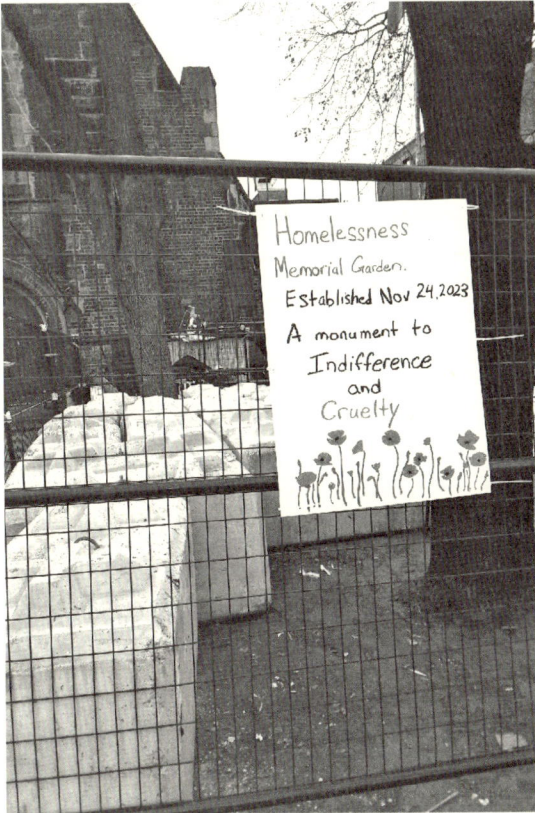

Homelessness
Memorial Garden.
Established Nov 24, 2023
A monument to
Indifference
and
Cruelty

could not be located, so his body was released to me. As I always do in these situations, I immediately phoned Rosar-Morrison, a funeral home of exceptional compassion and inclusivity, at one time the only funeral home that would handle people who died of HIV/AIDS, now the place more committed than any other to ensuring that people who die without housing are given respect and care. Because only next of kin can authorize cremation, a burial was required, but Rosar-Morrison managed to find an affordable plot at a cemetery within reach by TTC, on a small rise above a gravel path, with trees around it. It was a quiet place, attractive, peaceful, all the things Douglas had so rarely in his life. Isaac was one of the pallbearers; the others were some of our drop-in volunteers. It was something I had known for so many years would eventually fall to me that it seemed like it must mark the conclusion to something, but really, very few things except human lives actually conclude, and lives, as I have told the bereaved many times, always end in the middle of the story. Most of the narratives we create are deceptions.

Around this time my own life was entering a different and very bleak stage, as my husband's cognitive decline continued to escalate, and we eventually received a sort of diagnosis of 'dementia, cause unknown' (later on, it would become a formal diagnosis of Alzheimer's disease, missing the official cut-off for 'early onset' by a few months). In mid-January, he had a seizure in the middle of the night; I woke to find him flat on his back, seizing, choking on his own mucus and saliva, and if I had not been there to roll him onto his side he might have died then. I called a neighbour to come and sit with my daughter, rode with him in an ambulance to Toronto Western, and he couldn't remember his address or his date of birth. Although he would recover in part, his confusion was now so constant that I couldn't leave him, or my daughter, alone, and suddenly I was no longer able to be around the church or the encampment, to be available for unscheduled needs or random conversations. Even with support from the diocese for a few hours of home care every week, I was dashing in and out, on a strict schedule, unable to get to know new people, to set any kind of tone, most of my time at home with two dependent needy adults – and this is not that story, but it is a backdrop that can't be avoided any longer.

I told some of the people around the encampment, because they are part of my life, because they needed to know why I wasn't around as much anymore, and because I knew they would be kind. The Artist, who still came to the drop-in every Friday, frowned softly and made suggestions about vitamins and supplements. 'Because he shouldn't have to go through this. I mean, you're both metahumans, like me, so it shouldn't have to happen.' It was happening, and no vitamins were going to change it, but somehow, the fact that she included both of us in a magical category with herself was, for me, a true deep comfort.

❦

We started to hear rumours, on the coldest nights, that there were buses parked at Spadina station, on board which people were allowed to sleep. At the end of January, the *Toronto Star* broke the story officially. The buses, which had originally been intended to transport people to shelters or warming centres, had nowhere they could take anyone. So the TTC quietly, humanely, decided to do what small thing they could, and allowed the buses to become nighttime shelters. At the time when the *Toronto Star* story ran, they had recorded 1,072 overnight stays on the buses, and just 92 cases where they were able to take people to some more adequate shelter.

By the end of the season, when Shelter Services presented their plan for the next winter, the buses were public and official, part of the City's actual 'winter response' for 2024–25. The Anglican Diocese of Toronto has been asking, since then, why this is in any way a superior solution to opening warming centres in one or more of the churches that were rejected, but there has not yet been an answer to that question.

The Cecil Street Community Centre did manage to be accepted as an overflow site on the coldest days, but would reach capacity almost immediately each time. On one of those very cold days, in late February, the City issued a press release stating that Cecil would be closed to new admissions that night because there was no more room. The release also stated that City staff 'continue to connect with people living outside to encourage them to come indoors.' They did not explain how they could succeed in encouraging people to come indoors when there was no indoors for them to come into, except, if they were very lucky, an empty seat on a stationary bus at Spadina station.

❦

Already, in the fall of 2023, we had seen a new group around the encampment – very young women, in their teens. Smart, suspicious, most or all of them survivors of unspeakable abuse that began for them in childhood, heavy users of fentanyl long before they were legally allowed to drink, trying to tamp down the horrors. The older men in the tents would come to me and beg me to find someone who could 'get those girls off the street, *please*, Pastor,' and I would phone youth workers and counsellors, but none of the pieces seemed to connect.

One of them I met late on a Sunday night, after a service of Evensong, when two workers, needing to clock off their shifts, came into the church and handed her over to me until a crisis team could be located to pick her up and take her somewhere she would be unable to kill herself that night, keep her alive till sunrise. While we sat talking on the steps, she told me that while she had tried to kill herself three times in the last forty-eight hours, but while she had been sitting in the chapel, listening to the singing, she had felt almost peaceful. The next day I, and the TNG peer workers, and the nurse from ICHA, had a kind of rolling on-site case conference, and one of the peers eventually convinced her to sign a consent form so they could start looking for housing and supports for her. The nurse called up her history on his phone, and of course could tell me nothing, but I stood by the fence while he scrolled, murmuring, 'Oh, shit. Oh, no. Oh, *no.*'

None of the girls stayed in one place long, they came and went, separately more than together, hard to find, hard to connect with help. The one who had been brought to Evensong was in and out of hospital constantly, and often disappeared between admissions. In March, she started spending more consistent time around the encampment, often in the company of the relatively stable Pirate. I saw her at the drop-in one night, looking calmer and more focused than usual, and she told me she was doing well.

That was on a Friday. The next Wednesday was unnaturally, even bizarrely, hot for the time of year, a strange day, part of a frighteningly warm early spring. We were trying to deal with a round of harassment by bylaw, someone phoning in constant complaints to the City and triggering half a dozen potential notices of violation against the church, everything from the presence of rats in the yard to the condition of our eaves-troughs. At a meeting of the parish leadership, we agreed that communications between us and the City around garbage pickup were never going to be sufficient to get cleaning properly done. The Friday before, I had also talked to the Artist, who was spending more of her time at the encampment nearer to the lake, but still had a tent at our site which she sometimes used. She told me that she had emotionally released her latest collection of rescued trash, which was spreading like an oil spill out over the sidewalk, and we needed to act while we could, so we booked a junk removal company for Thursday, when I knew I would have a five-hour block of respite care and didn't have to be at home.

I pulled up on my bicycle on Thursday just after 11 a.m., planning to work in the kitchen for an hour before the cleanup volunteers arrived, but I saw one of the community police officers standing in the south walkway, near Robin's tent, looking subdued in a way that wasn't normal, so I leaned my bike against the fence and asked him if everything was okay.

'We've got an overdose,' he said. 'It's confirmed.' It took a few rounds of miscommunication before I understood that 'confirmed' meant 'dead.' Female, he said. In the tent just a couple of feet along the path from Robin. The last person I'd known to be in that tent was a man, but tent occupancy is often fluid. He offered to open the tent so that I could try to identify the person.

It was a small tent, one of the single-person models. Inside, a body in a crouch, bent forward, face pressed into the ground-sheet. I couldn't see enough to be sure of anything. Another officer came over, and they carefully moved the body out of the tent, laid her on her back. She had been dead for a while. Her face was bloated, distorted, patches of cold white and congested blue. Her head had been recently shaved. I thought it was the girl from Evensong, and I thought, no, it isn't, and I just wasn't sure. I walked away and tried to call Andrew, but only got voice mail. Then I walked back.

'I need to do my job now,' I said to the officer.

'Yes,' he said. 'Just don't touch anything.'

I knelt beside the body, holding my hand above her forehead, and said the prayers for the dead. A few more officers arrived while I was doing this, and I heard one of them saying, 'Who's that, should she be here?'

'I'm the priest,' I said. That seemed to be enough.

It occurred to me now, as it should have earlier, that I should talk to the people living nearby. But Robin was away for the morning, as they often were, having breakfast at the TNG drop-in. I woke Pirate, and he climbed out of his makeshift shed.

'Oh my God,' he said. 'I think that's the girl … she's wearing the belt I gave her yesterday.'

And somehow, the angle, and maybe the fact that she'd been turned over so that some of the distortion of her face settled down, meant I could recognize her now. It was that same girl. This time she had not made it through the night. The paramedics came, and they knew her, too. The community officer gently pulled her hat down to cover her face.

I phoned Andrew again and reached him. 'I went to the encampment to look for her last night,' he said. 'But I couldn't find her.' Probably, we agreed, she had already been dead in the tent.

And then cleanup volunteers started to arrive, and we had to go ahead with that plan, everything already booked and organized, though luckily only for the north plot. The police taped off an area that included Robin's tent, so I had to phone around to find someone who could locate them and tell them they wouldn't be able to come home for a little while. Pirate sat on the steps wracked with guilt because he hadn't been watching her that night, because he'd alienated her by telling her she was using too much, because she died using alone.

And for the next four hours, we hauled garbage that City workers had refused to touch, though much of it was on the property the City claims as its own, while the girl's body lay on the path a few yards away, watched over by a special constable. The coroner arrived, examined the scene, and announced that he wanted a forensic team in. It started to rain while she was lying there waiting for the forensics unit, there was nothing we could do, processes are unchangeable, but we didn't want her to lie there in the rain, she had been out in the rain too long, too often.

My home-care hours ran out before the cleanup was finished, and before she was taken away, and I had no choice but to leave. I was on the phone with my colleague Andrea a few hours later, when forensics had come and gone, and the last vehicle finally arrived. Andrea and Andrew – along with Dominique, a community activist who had been passing by and realized what was happening – stood by to see her lifted up from the walkway. Andrea said the prayers I wasn't there to say.

The next day Andrew and I cleaned out the tent in which she had died, while Robin cried softly in a chair beside us. Although it had not been the girl's tent exactly, it didn't seem right to leave it to be destroyed by weather and neglect. I salvaged two good candleholders from the wreckage, and we lit small candles where the tent had stood.

While we were folding tarps and pouring out collected rainwater, we were approached by another girl, even younger, a thin girl with glasses who was sharing a derelict tent with someone else, who wanted to know if this one was still in decent shape. We helped her set it up on a clear spot on the north plot, told her this tent was meant just for her, reminded her that we were there to talk if she needed us, and that there were other good and reliable people around her. And, most immediately, that if she used fentanyl, which she told us she did, she should make very sure not to use alone, always to have someone who was watching. I knew something about this girl's story, too, the history of abuse, the forms that took her in and out of hospital, the friends lost to toxic drugs, the handful of people in her life who cared about her and were trying to do their best. The same story, with inflections of detail, so many times, for each distinct and precise person, each loss, each name.

The Artist reappeared, looked at the cleared north plot – just three tents, with bare earth around them – and said, 'Looks good!' Then she immediately headed to the garbage bins of the apartment complex next door, pulled out not one but two rocking horses, and carried them over to us.

❧

It became clear, as the fence stayed up, that it was actually a safety hazard, that it made putting up curtained areas and visual barriers so easy and removed the high visibility that had been one of our important characteristics. Along with the damage to trust and relationships, and the disruption of consistent patterns and long-term residents, it made it more likely that any given day would bring a serious incident. In April, my worst fear about the stairwell came true, when someone – not an encampment resident, and we never learned his name – was found down there past reviving, perhaps in part because there were no clear sight lines to that area anymore, and no one close at hand able to notice and respond. We had fewer tents but more fires, although never any that ran out of control like the fire of the previous spring.

Some of the people who had gone into shelter-hotels on that day in November had come back to the church by now, 'restricted' according to the usual pattern, for reasons sufficiently trivial that they sometimes didn't even know what the reasons were. Others were now in other encampments; there were more tents in Bellevue Square Park again, a larger and slightly less exposed location, not policed as vigorously as it had been the last two years. And the encampment south of Queen Street had rapidly grown into one of the largest in the city.

On May 22, 2024, the City released a new 'interdivisional protocol for encampments.' A reporter from the CBC came to the church to get a comment from me. As I arrived at the church with my daughter, I noticed the smell of smoke, but also saw a pile of trash, obviously charred, sitting at the curb, so I assumed that yet another fire had just happened, and been extinguished. Then I saw Emerald, a small, fragile, intensely emotional woman who had flitted for years between our encampment and several others, before obtaining housing, in what was meant to be a supportive housing complex, a couple of months earlier, one of our very few housing victories. She was carrying a document in front of her in a metal sieve, and asked me to take it and read it to her. 'I don't want to touch it,' she said. 'It's an eviction letter. I just need to know what date I have to be out.'

She had to be out, according to the document, by the end of June. The reason given was excessive clutter and debris in her unit, and some kind of water leakage. There was a three-page narrative account attached, and if her 'supportive housing worker' had offered any meaningful support beyond reprimands, it was not recorded in that account. Mental health specialists and hoarding specialists had not been involved, at least according to what was written in the eviction order.

Although the form included a line for actions she could take to prevent the eviction, that line was blank. In a final flourish, she was required to pay the $185 cost of the eviction notice. She would be back on the street by July, unless she decided to cut her losses by leaving earlier.

I sent my daughter into the church, and the reporter arrived. While we were shooting the post-interview filler footage – me walking into the church, me walking out of the church, and so on – an older homeless man came running up to me, anxiously calling out, 'Reverend, I'm so sorry to interrupt, but you should know there's a fire at the back of the church. I tried to put it out as best I could, but you better take a look.' Then he dashed off again. I followed him, and around the back I found a pile of cardboard in flames, and this one old man stomping up and down on the fire as it grew rapidly. Pounding on the door until Janet opened it, I grabbed a fire extinguisher, fumbled with the plug, and eventually discharged a huge cloud of chemicals, all under the camera gaze of the CBC.

When I went back inside, I learned that there were half a dozen police cars on Augusta Avenue, for reasons never made clear to anyone, but I later heard several stories of a person setting piles of cardboard on fire around the Market, and some-one, the same person or another, doing the same in the Gay Village. I also learned that, because someone had phoned a different CBC reporter, and also multiple City departments, to complain that our belltower was 'going to fall down and kill someone,' we were getting a visit from two City inspectors that same day. They arrived later; one of them suggested that 'maybe the CBC could give you repair money,' and we were served, the next day, with an order to have an engineer deliver a full report on all the brickwork to the City by the next week, at our expense.

On Sunday, as we were serving coffee and cookies in the yard, Emerald showed up, wearing black, her head shaved, and told me she didn't want us to try to fight the eviction, didn't want to go back, didn't want to live indoors anymore, that this was a sign that she just couldn't do it and shouldn't even try. I was barely able get her to take at least a chocolate biscuit.

As for the encampment strategy, it was, as I had anticipated, essentially an arrangement of words, some expressions of hope without much foundation, and a repetition of limited promises mostly already made, like the creation of 1,600 additional shelter spaces over the next decade – nothing in the paper likely to cause immediate harm, and nothing in it suggesting any concrete reasons to expect any positive change.

❦

When I looked out into my pocket backyard at home in the mornings that spring, I was aware of seeing far fewer birds, aware that the dawn chorus was less dense and varied. Some sparrows, but not even as many of those. Not many gulls, maybe one robin. No cardinals, goldfinches, or jays. Now and then, the sound of a woodpecker. It is anecdotal, I cannot prove that this is the devastation of avian flu or anything to do with climate change, but I know the world is becoming more poor, more thin.

Still, at the church, as I walked around in preparation for a visit from a structural engineer, I saw two adolescent starlings, nesting in one of the crevices around our front door. It wasn't good for the brickwork, and luckily they were out looking for food when the engineer arrived, but the sight of them made it a good day.

The engineer's report, paid for by the diocese in the end, found the bricks adequately sound, just as every previous building inspection had. The harassment through bylaws receded for a while. But the forbidding fence and concrete blocks, the fear of what could happen to tents on City property, the frequent inspections by police, fire services, and the Encampment Office, the sense of shattered community, and my own inability to be present, all these things meant that people continued to drift elsewhere. Finally, only Robin and Pirate remained as permanent residents, though others sometimes came and went. Bellevue Square Park was filled with tents, including many of the people who had been regulars at the church encampment, and by summer someone started circulating a petition with the odd, and clearly committee-generated, demand that the City forcibly relocate the encampment residents to dignified and affordable housing. More tents went up in Doctors' Parkette. Alexandra Park was fenced off for part of the summer for 'revitalization,' but within a week of its reopening I counted seven tents, and more came later.

Jeff reappeared in Bellevue Square Park, much thinner, pale, withdrawn, his speech low and almost inaudible, his attention wandering – the ambiguous loss of Taurus a trauma from which he hasn't been able to recover, which has activated other traumas, left him unmoored. But still the same warmth in his eyes when he greeted me.

At the beginning of July, after months of official silence, the pressure against our last two residents suddenly escalated again. We were given an ultimatum – not the first or the last – for Robin and Pirate to remove any of their things that were on the lawn or the walkways, or face unspecified consequences.

On Thursday, I waved at Robin as I pulled out on my bike in the late afternoon, and they waved back from where they were working on a blue-green abstract painting. Within a few hours, Andrew had texted me to say that Robin had suddenly been arrested. He had passed the church and found them sitting, hands cuffed behind their back, surrounded by police officers, and he followed them to 14 Division, and for a long time no one would tell him anything, but then one of the community officers happened to walk in and gave him the information for how to be in Zoom court the next day.

That Friday morning, after a gruelling two-hour appointment, I signed papers to put my husband on a waiting list for a long-term care home – and then spent the rest of the day in Zoom court, along with Andrew, where we learned that the arrest had been an essentially arbitrary decision to enforce a series of bench warrants for failure to appear in court, tracking back to an offence allegedly committed almost two full years earlier. I am prepared to believe that the timing of the arrest may have been coincidental. Andrew does not agree.

Neither of us had standing with the court, of course. And it seemed for a while that Robin would be held over the weekend at least, sent from 14 Division to a distant jail, traumatized again. But we managed, between us, to create enough of a nuisance, as the case was traversed from court to court, that duty counsel agreed to meet with us and try to come up with a solution, and the Crown, astonishingly, agreed to it, and Robin was released that night, with Andrew as surety, because his criminal record is shorter than mine.

'Thank you,' said the justice of the peace, as we wrapped up, 'for caring so much about your friend.' As if this was something that never happened. Because, of course, it mostly never does, most people don't have friends with the privilege and the confidence to keep politely disrupting the court until they get what they want.

We met the ultimatum. And then there were other ultimatums, about other areas, or other belongings, and Robin kept moving their tent around according to arcane rules of their own understanding, which were not necessarily the rules of the fire service or the Department of Transportation.

On August 1, after nearly a year of silence, Mr. Holly phoned me at 7 a.m., with no acknowledgement that this was a strange hour for a business call, to tell me that there would be 'a garbage pickup' that day. Just a regular garbage pickup, he said. They might take a few of the big pieces of wood that were lying in the yard. I asked him why he was phoning me at 7 a.m. if it was just a regular garbage pickup. 'Well, because it's, like, a different day than usual, you know? Because of the long weekend? But nothing crazy, okay? Just a garbage pickup.'

I cannot say that I felt reassured. But my husband's PSW was not arriving until eleven, and it didn't seem possible to text my volunteers at 7 a.m. to say that the City said they were going to do a garbage pickup but it just felt wrong.

Later that morning, sometime before I arrived, City crews came and took *everything*, on church property as well as City property. Robin's tent, tarps, people's personal belongings. Half of Pirate's lean-to against the church wall was taken apart, and the rest was probably only left because the intricacy of the construction defeated the crew. The yard was barren, scraped earth, emptier than I had ever seen it. Robin had retreated to the back garden, Pirate to the stairwell.

They regrouped, they found new materials, they were not going to leave their home. Andrew and I did everything we could to assure Robin that they were safe, at least as safe as we could manage. But it is a fingernail of space now.

❦

Is it a story of defeat, then, in the end? To the extent that we were not able to preserve the churchyard as a place of sanctuary, I suppose it is. The stability that people achieved there has been lost for at least some, Jeff perhaps most of all, and almost everyone is still living in an encampment, just in a different one. And certainly, neither we nor anyone else has been able to turn around a vast political and economic system that is more and more devoted to protecting the wealth of a very few, as most people, and the planet as a whole, fall deeper into chaos.

But that we – the church, the encampment residents, the 'we' that is all of us – held that space for more than two years is not nothing. And Robin is there still, their future as uncertain as ever, but their fragile stability persisting. They still decorate their area with potted plants retrieved from garbage, they still do their paintings, they are slight and evanescent as the wind, but they are here. The Artist comes to see us every Friday, offers me her news from the universe and her cosmic comforts, and stays on after midnight to clean up and weed the open part of the yard.

Douglas, one of the hardest people to like whom I've ever met, was never wholly alone, had times of peace and safety, and he died with friends around him, and was buried with dignity, by the community he had chosen. Isaac trusts us, now that his family doctor has retired, to tell him when he needs his meds, and lets us accompany him to the hospital or the pharmacy to get his Invega shot; and he comes several times a week to evening prayer, sometimes brings a friend, finds comfort and protection in the old words of the Book of Common Prayer.

One Saturday in early August, as we were setting up for an outdoor service in Bellevue Square Park, Jeff asked me, 'Do you remember that ship we built? Like, the time we built that ship in the churchyard, out of wooden skids, remember?' I didn't remember exactly such a thing, but Jeff had created any number of constructions, so I nodded.

'Well,' he said, almost whispering, 'I heard that they dug it up two million years in the future. And it was completely the same. It was perfect. That's pretty amazing, isn't it?'

'It is,' I said. 'It really is.'

'Two million years in the future. Just think about it. That ship we built, completely the same.'

And while we may not have built a ship out of wooden skids exactly, we did build a little ark in the yard for a while, a place of refuge against the flood, a place where we preserved what we could.

In some unimaginable future, somewhere the other side of the coming floods and the fire next time, will someone remember it? Will someone dig it up and find it still perfect? I cannot say that this may not be true.

In memoriam:

AJ Ballard, Luc Boulienne, Brandon, Dishon Shannon
Brooks ('Mama'), Robert Frederick Carson, Summer Cowen,
Selim Esen, Faye, Ashton Darnell 'Pikachu' Gray,
Chris Hussin, Ice-Man, Charlene Lee, Dean Lisowick, Don
'Turtle' Motrick, Xavier Mason Anthony Osborne-Hofstede,
Kevin Parker, Dave Vasey;

Leroy Granville Francis Niles;

David Gordon Helwig

The bodies are all accounted for

Notes

All quotations from Rowan Williams are from his epilogue to *Praying for England: Priestly Presence in Contemporary Culture*, edited by Samuel Wells and Sarah Coakley (Continuum Press, 2008). The hymn verses beginning 'Sacred infant, all divine' on page 32 are taken from 'See amid the winter's snow' by Edward Caswall, originally published in *The Masque of Mary and other poems* (Burns and Lambert, 1858) and reprinted in many hymnals. The quotation on page 65 from John Donne is taken from his Holy Sonnet 'At the round earth's imagined corners' (Sonnet 7 in the 1912 Grierson edition). The quotation on page 65 from T. S. Eliot is taken from *Ash Wednesday* (Faber and Faber, 1930).

A version of the chapter 'Disappearance' was previously published in *Brick*.

Image Credits

p. 5. illustration by Sasha Tate-Howarth; p. 31. photograph by Maggie Helwig; p. 58. photograph by Michael Hudson; p. 102. photograph by Andrew Neelands; p. 114. photograph by Michael Hudson; p. 167. photograph by Michael Longfield; p. 170. photograph by Dominique Russell; p. 175. photograph by Maggie Helwig; p. 193. photograph by Michael Hudson

Acknowledgements

My very deep thanks to all those encampment residents, and other marginalized people in our community, who have shared their stories with me. Thanks most of all to Jeff, Robin, Pirate, and the Artist, our longest-term residents, who agreed to be interviewed for this book, and trusted me to write about our shared experiences. We were a major part of each other's lives for two years or more, and I can only hope that I have enriched their lives even half as much as they have mine. As Robin wisely pointed out, no one can ever fully understand another person's experience, so this book reflects my experience and my perspective only, but I hope it at least honours and does not falsify theirs.

Thanks as well to everyone from the parish who understood immediately that this was what we had to do, all the people who cook and serve meals, unclog toilets, provide first aid, have conversations, de-escalate conflicts, talk people off the ledge (sometimes literally), and generally keep everything running during crisis after crisis, including many not mentioned in the text – especially Andrea Budgey, who was there from the beginning of everything, and Janet Nichols, Elizabeth Cummings, John Spragge (who gave me the goal of 'alive at sunrise'), Tucker Gordon, Louis Bursey, Esther Townshend, the late Leroy Niles, Cera Cruise, Noah Lamanna, Max Price, and our outstanding volunteer community worker Andrew Neelands.

Thank you to all those at the Diocese of Toronto who have supported us, especially Bishop Andrew Asbil, Bishop Kevin Robertson, Canon Rob Saffrey, Mac Moreau, and the incomparable Elin Goulden. Special thanks to now-retired Bishop

Philip Poole, the risk-seeking bishop who first placed me at St. Stephen's, agreed to let me open the church overnight with no clear plan, and chatted with me on my cellphone while Andrea and I were bike-locked to a railing in the lobby of a TD bank.

Thanks to our friends in Kensington Market, including Dominique Russell, Sylvia Lassam, Serena Purdy, Su Alexanian, and many others. A particular note of thanks to Irene Morales at Jumbo Empanadas, who almost single-handedly supplied hot dinners for the people seeking shelter at the Metro Hall warming centre in the winter of 2014. Thanks to Samara Secter and Jocelyn Rempel at Addario Law, who handled our application for an injunction to protect the encampment, and to sympathetic journalists including Dale Manucdoc at CBC Toronto, Chris Young at Canadian Press, Victoria Gibson at the *Toronto Star*, Shaughnessy Bishop-Stall at the *Globe and Mail*, Joanna Lavoie at CTV/Global, Ian Wilms at the Hoser, Sam Rosati Martin at the Local, and many others.

Thank you to everyone at Alexandra Community Encampment Support, Voices for Unhoused Liberation, the Apple Crisp Action Brigade, and to Diana Chan McNally, to the wonderful Lowe Goldsmith, and to many others. And more thanks than I can express to our colleagues at The Neighbourhood Group, including Tina Estwick, Amber Kellen, Marquito Lee Free, Caryn O'Brien, Barb Panter, Lydia Rezene, Bill Sinclair, Lorie Steer, Nadia Wali, and all the peer workers, whose support of the encampment residents has been consistent and invaluable.

Thank you to TinyKittens Society of Langley, BC, for a model of what compassionate care for all creatures should be.

Thanks to Erika Peterson and Rachel Manija Brown, who read the manuscript in draft and made useful suggestions. I am grateful to Natalie Fingerhut from U of T Press for first suggesting that I write this book, and for being gracious about my decision not to publish it with U of T Press. I am also grateful to all those who commissioned the shorter pieces that would become part of this book, including Dr. Nili Kaplan-Myrth (editor of *Breaking Canadians*), Stuart Mann at *The Anglican*, and Matthew Halliday at *Maclean's*.

And, of course, thanks to Alana Wilcox, the best editor in Canada, and everyone else at Coach House Books.

My husband, Ken Simons, is no longer able to read this book or these acknowledgements. But his many years of support, and unpaid caregiving for our daughter, are the only reason that I have been able to do the things that I have done out in the world. I hope that he can still understand that I am grateful.

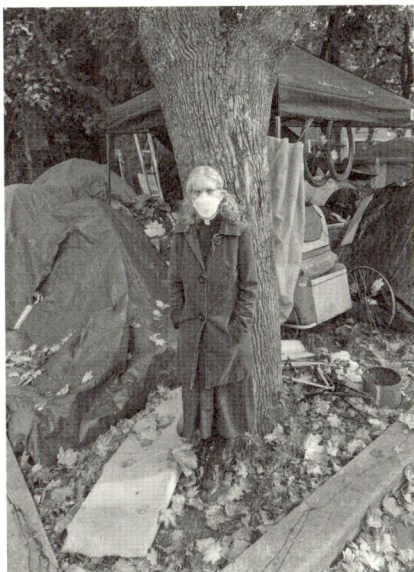

Maggie Helwig (she/they) is a white settler in Tkaronto/ Toronto, and is the author of fifteen books and chapbooks, most recently *Girls Fall Down* (Coach House, 2008), which was shortlisted for the Toronto Book Award, and was chosen as the One Book Toronto in 2012. Helwig is a long-time social justice activist, and also an Anglican priest, and has been the rector of the Church of St. Stephen-in-the-Fields since 2013.

Typeset in Arno and IvyPresto.

Printed at the Coach House on bpNichol Lane in Toronto, Ontario, on FSC-certified Sustana recycled paper, which was manufactured in Saint-Jérôme, Quebec. This book was printed with vegetable-based ink on a 1973 Heidelberg KORD offset litho press. Its pages were folded on a Baumfolder, gathered by hand, bound on a Sulby Auto-Minabinda, and trimmed on a Polar single-knife cutter.

Coach House Books, and the Church of St. Stephen-in-the-Fields, are situated on occupied land, the traditional territory of several Indigenous nations, including the Mississaugas of the Credit (an Anishnabek people), the Haudenosaunee Confederacy, and the Wendat and Petun nations, and now home to many First Nations, Inuit, and Métis people. This land is covered by the Dish With One Spoon Covenant, an agreement between different First Nations communities to share resources peacefully and equitably, and by the Two-Row Wampum, a covenant of mutual respect and non-interference between early settlers and the Haudenosaunee. The land is also subject to Treaty 13, sometimes called the Toronto Purchase, signed between the settler colonists and the Mississaugas of the Credit.

As settler organizations, we acknowledge that we have violated these treaties and agreements. We acknowledge the grievous and ongoing harm of colonialism, and we acknowledge that the Anglican Church played a significant role in this. We strive to work toward a future of justice and reconciliation.

Edited by Alana Wilcox
Cover and interior design by Crystal Sikma
Cover and author photo by Michael Hudson

Coach House Books
80 bpNichol Lane
Toronto ON M5S 3J4
Canada
mail@chbooks.com
www.chbooks.com